WAL
A

Atlantic coast near Arrifana (Walk 26)

WALKING IN THE ALGARVE

by
June Parker

June Parker 4.6.1997

CICERONE PRESS
MILNTHORPE, CUMBRIA

ISBN 1 85284 173 7
A catalogue record for this book is available from the British Library.

ACKNOWLEDGEMENTS

The author is particularly grateful to Rita and Mike Gallie for introducing her to the Algarve, their help in finding walks and their company on many of them. Thanks also to Chris and Ken Bricknell for help in identification of flowers and to David Ormerod for contributing Walk No 7. Special thanks of course to Alan Parker for all his help in the compilation of this book.

Front cover: Top - Ponta de Telheiro (Walk 30)
Bottom - Windmill near Azinhal. (Walk 23)

CONTENTS

WALKING ROUTES

Western area

Eastern area

ADVICE TO READERS

Readers are advised that whilst every effort is taken by the author to ensure the accuracy of this guidebook, changes can occur which may affect the contents. A book of this nature with detailed descriptions and detailed maps is more prone to change than a more general guide. New fences and stiles appear, waymarking alters, there may be new buildings or eradication of old buildings. It is advisable to check locally on transport, accommodation, shops etc. but even rights-of-way can be altered, paths can be eradicated by landslip, forest clearances or changes of ownership. The publisher would welcome notes of any such changes.

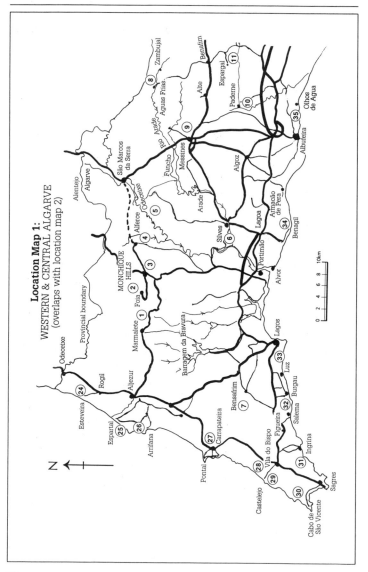

Location Map 1:
WESTERN & CENTRAL ALGARVE
(overlaps with location map 2)

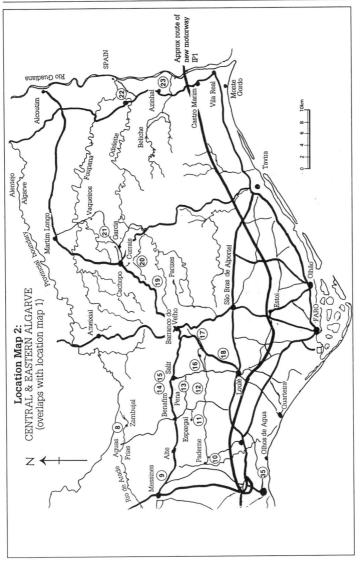

Location Map 2:
CENTRAL & EASTERN ALGARVE
(overlaps with location map 1)

Olhos de Agua (Walk 35)

INTRODUCTION

The area of southern Portugal known as the Algarve has been a destination for winter sunseekers for many years. Although it is bordered by the Atlantic ocean it is warmed by the Gulf stream and has a Mediterranean climate with hot dry summers and mild and sunny winters. The coastline is spectacular with high cliffs and dramatic rock scenery including blowholes, hundreds of tiny rocky islands and sea-stacks, rock archways and bridges sculpted by the sea and beaches and coves with clean yellow sand.

Part of the appeal for walkers is the miles of walking along the cliff tops, but inland too there are granite mountains up to 900m and lower limestone hills featuring escarpments and caves. Further north there are deeply dissected *matos*-covered hills with an acid soil where there are few cultivated areas. There are small villages completely untouched by tourism, offering glimpses of a way of life that will soon disappear. Water is collected in large ceramic jars on the back of a mule, washing is still done at public washplaces and sometimes in the river. The scenery is not dramatic except at the coast, but full of interest for walkers, especially those with an interest in wild flowers, agriculture and birds. In January and February millions of almond trees come into flower, producing beautiful blossoms in profusion and before the leaves appear, so that whole hillsides have a pink and white glow. In the orange groves the trees are laden with fruit and the fertile ground produces many crops of all kinds of vegetables.

Recent years have seen a massive increase in tourist development, so that some of the old fishing villages have become large resorts spoilt by unrestricted growth of hotels and villas. Fortunately steps have now been taken to protect areas of natural beauty and these include all of the Western Atlantic coastline where some of the best coastal walks are found, Monchique in the area of the highest mountains, the Rocha de Pena and the Fonte de Benémola in the Barrocal limestone area and the banks of the river Arade near Silves and the Rio Guadiana on the Spanish border. A nature reserve has been created near Faro, preserving an important wetland area where there are many unique species of plants and animals. Another is to be found at Castro Marim in the east where a flock of flamingoes is one of the attractions.

WHERE TO STAY

The Algarve measures some 160km (100 miles) from east to west and averages about 30km from north to south. The cheapest way of staying there is to book a package holiday with one of the major tour operators. Staying somewhere near Albufeira which is roughly in the centre means it is possible to cover the whole area, provided you have a car. Lagos in the west is also recommended. It is an attractive old town between Albufeira and Sagres and cliff-top walks can be done directly or by using local transport. Another option would be to book a fly-drive package. There are always rooms to let in small villages, advertised by the sign 'Quartos' and often 'rooms', 'chambres' and 'zimmer'. This has the advantage of avoiding the overdeveloped tourist resorts and giving greater freedom of movement.

CAMPING

There is a large international campsite near Albufeira which is open all winter. Other *Parques de campismo* open all winter are at Aljezur, Armação de Pera, Faro, Ingrina and Lagos. A camping guidebook *Roteiro Campista* can be obtained from the Portugese Tourist Office in London or from tourist offices and bookshops in the Algarve. Camping away from official sites is not allowed and is strictly forbidden on all beaches.

GETTING ABOUT

Car hire is cheap in the winter months which are the best time for walking and in the winters of 1992 and 1993 it was possible to obtain a package deal which included a free hire car for the whole stay. This may not always be the case, but it is worth looking for special deals which give cheap car hire rates. At first driving seems hazardous, especially along the main east-west route, the EN125. This is because local drivers continually exceed the speed limit and are notorious for dangerous overtaking. As soon as this road is left for the quieter country roads leading to the hills it is a different story and there is no problem, except for watching out for the continually forming potholes and trenches. A new stretch of motorway, the IP1, which runs from near Albufeira to the Spanish border, has made getting about much easier. Similarly the road from Lagos to Cabo de São Vicente is being widened and when completed this will make all journeys to the west far quicker. Using public transport to get to the start of the walks is not really an option, except at Lagos as already mentioned. There are buses to Burgau and Sagres in the west and up to Monchique in the highest mountain area. However, it takes a long time, about 2 hours, with a change of bus in Portimão, and hiring a car is preferable.

WEATHER AND CLIMATE

The Algarve has one of the best climates in the whole of Europe with an average of 3000 hours of sunshine every year and an average annual temperature of 17°C. The summers are long, hot and dry and cloudless blue skies can be guaranteed day after day. The average maximum August temperature is 29.7°C, which is too hot for walking for most people. On the other hand the relative humidity is low so that the heat does not feel unduly oppressive. In the clear atmosphere there is a real danger of sunburn in the summer months, making barrier suncreams and headcoverings essential. Even the winter sun can be strong enough to make protection necessary for some people. *Algarvios* have always recognised this and can be seen wearing hats and scarves or taking refuge under black umbrellas.

We found the winter months of January, February and March perfect for walking with a midday temperature varying between 16 and 23°C. Similar temperatures were found in November and December. It is much cooler first thing in the morning and when the sun goes down. On one occasion we encountered a frost pocket where at 10.00 the temperature was only 8°C, but this rose rapidly to 15°C by lunch time. Another time thin sheets of ice were observed on some narrow north-facing terraces where watercress was being grown, but this was exceptional. Besides being cooler in the hills there is a temperature gradient between east and west and it is noticeably cooler at Sagres and Cape St Vincent. This western area also has stronger winds and more overcast days than elsewhere.

Rainfall is unpredictable, except for its absence in July and August. Most of the annual rain occurs some time between May and October but there is no knowing exactly when. When it does rain it is likely to be torrential but afterwards to clear up very quickly. On such days it is better to spend the time shopping, reading, visiting museums or exploring some of the interesting old towns. The Algarve is undoubtedly an ideal destination for a quiet and peaceful walking holiday, especially when Britain is in the grips of a grey and depressing winter.

Shrubby pimpernel

GEOLOGY AND SCENERY

The relationship between the scenery and the underlying rock structure is clearly evident in the Algarve. There are three distinct areas, each with characteristic topography and vegetation. These areas are (1) the northern shale mountains, (2) the central limestone hills and (3) the southern coastal zone of mixed sedimentary rocks and recent deposits. In addition there is a plutonic intrusion in the northern shales and a narrow contact zone between areas (1) and (2). These will each be described below.

NORTHERN SHALES

In the northern part of the Algarve is a large mountainous area of carboniferous shales covering two-thirds of the province and forming a natural boundary with the rest of Portugal. These mountains top 500m in places and are interrupted only by the San Marcos depression through which run road and rail links from Albufeira to the north. These mountains form a rolling landscape with long high ridges and deeply dissected valleys. Formerly they were thickly forested with both cork oak and holm oak, but whole areas were stripped of tree cover during the fifteenth century when oak was wanted for shipbuilding during the Portuguese voyages of discovery. One consequence of this was that discarded trimmings and loose soil were washed downslope in winter rains, leading to the silting up of river estuaries and to further erosion of the land. During the first world war, further deforestation occured in attempts to grow more wheat. Although this was successful at first, yields rapidly diminished owing to the shallow topsoil. The picture today is one of a fairly barren landscape still supporting coak oaks among the natural scrub or *matos* with small villages and isolated farms still growing some cereals, vegetables and fruit or raising goats.

The carboniferous shales are well exposed on the cliffs of the Atlantic coast and can be seen on all of the walks in this area, from 24 to 30.

MONCHIQUE MOUNTAINS

In the north-west a plutonic intrusion of a granitic rock forms the

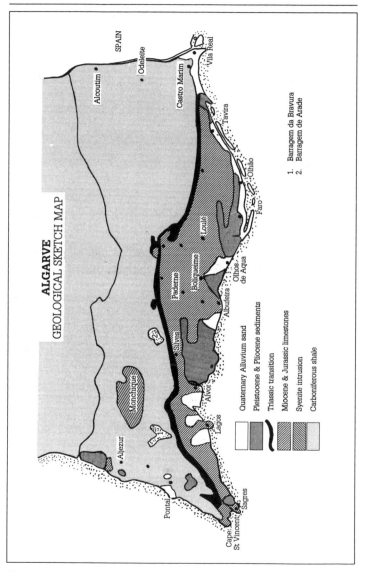

ALGARVE
GEOLOGICAL SKETCH MAP

Quaternary Alluvium sand

Pleistocene & Pliocene sediments

Triassic transition

Miocene & Jurassic limestones

Syenite intrusion

Carboniferous shale

1. Barragem da Bravura
2. Barragem de Arade

SPAIN

Alcoutim

Odeleite

Castro Marim

Vila Real

Tavira

Olhão

Faro

Olhos-
de Aqua

Loulé

Paderne

Boliqueime

Albufeira

Silves

Monchique

Alvor

Lagos

Aljezur

Pontal

Sagres

Cape
St Vincent

Serra de Monchique, where the high tops of Madrinha, Fóia and Picota are the highest in the Algarve, at 803m, 902m and 774m respectively. The rock has been named as Foyaite and is a very pale coarse type of nepheline syenite. It outcrops in many places and has been quarried near the town of Monchique which lies between Fóia and Picota. Some of these outcrops are seen on Walks 1, 2 and 3. The quarry lies next to the main road near the branch to Marmalete and is of an impressive size. Men still cut small blocks by hand for use in paving. These hills too are being forested in part by eucalyptus.

CONTACT ZONE

Separating the northern shales from the Barrocal limestone is a narrow contact zone made up of various rocks of Triassic age. Most striking of these is a dark red sandstone, used to build the large hill-top castle at Silves. This sandstone weathers to a deep red soil of considerable importance. Along the contact zone surface water running off the shale slopes percolates down into aquifers in the limestone. The zone is very fertile and supports a sizable population in a chain of small towns and villages. From west to east these are Vila do Bispo, Bensafrim, Silves, São Bart, Alte, Salir, Querença, São Bras and Santa Caterina. All these lie in a trough between the northern shale hills and the limestone.

THE BARROCAL LIMESTONE

The limestone hills lie in a lens-shaped area extending from Cape St Vincent in the west almost to the Spanish border in the east. It is widest in the central area, tapering off both east and west. The age of these limestones is from Jurassic to Miocene, which is an enormous period of geological time. Hence their chemical composition is extremely varied reflecting different conditions at the time of deposition. The purest limestones and dolomites were used to make quicklime for the whitewashing of houses which was done several times a year. A study of the topographic maps such as 50C, São Bras de Alportel will show large areas regularly dotted with limekilns. In fact the approximate geological boundaries can readily be inferred both from the presence of kilns and from the contours which show ridges and valleys in the shales and long flat-topped hills in the limestones. Many of these limestone hills form ridges parallel to the contact zone. Rocha de Pena at 480m is the highest of these and the most striking, with vertical cliffs on the north and the south meeting each other in the east. The cliffs on the south are the only ones providing any rock-climbing in the Algarve.

The word Barrocal (from barro = clay or land yielding clay and cal = lime) usually means a barren hilly landscape supporting only maquis-type vegetation, or a wasteland which cannot be cultivated. Nothing could be further from the truth in the case of the Algarvian Barrocal which is a highly productive area growing thousands of almonds, olives, figs, carobs and many other crops. The flora too is outstandingly diverse.

COASTAL ZONE

This area is generally below 200m and much of it below 70m. It is not flat, but gently undulating. It is a mixed zone with sedimentary rocks deposited on a bed of Pliocene limestones. These sediments are interspersed with more recent deposits of two different types. To the west of Faro, in the *Barlovento* as it is known (the windward side), there are alluvial deposits brought down by the major rivers Alvor and Arade. To the east of Faro in the *Sotovento*, or leeward side, there are coastal sands deposited by the ocean. Thus the southern coast is quite different west and east of Faro. The western part is characterised by high cliffs and very dramatic rock scenery including blowholes, rock arches and bridges. Beaches are small and of clean yellow sand. To the east of Faro there are long beaches of sand and gravel and a long chain of islands and sandspits. A lagoon of brackish water has formed and inland are areas of salt-marsh. Some of this has been drained and developed but much is now protected in the Ria Formosa Nature Park (*q.v.*). Some of the coastal cliffs are especially colourful, particularly where iron is present and green and red colouration reflects reducing and oxidising conditions at the time of deposition.

The coastal zone was almost entirely agricultural until twenty years ago. Now tourist developments have taken over large areas both as hotels and villas and as golf courses. West of Lagos the coast is spectacularly beautiful and almost unspoilt, as it is northwards from Cape St Vincent. At Cape St Vincent, a limestone pavement is exposed, transgressing on to the northern shales after a few kilometres. At Pontal, a massive headland is capped by some impressively large sand dunes.

WILD FLOWERS

The wide variety of soil types, diverse habitats and the mild and sunny climate all combine to produce an astonishing range of flowering plants and shrubs. These are at their best from February to June when the whole landscape is enriched by blazes of colour from the highest mountains to the coastal cliffs. Even during the high season of July and August when many plants are scorched and brown there are exceptions such as the sea daffodil and the bright reddish-purple flowers of the stemless thistle, *Atractylis gumnifera*. In September and October the flowering season begins again when the tall spikes of the sea squill, *Urginea maritima*, shoot up from their enormous bulbs before the leaves emerge. In late November we found some lovely paper-white narcissi high up near the top of Espargal, growing in a damp place on the north side of a rocky outcrop.

There are literally thousands of species to delight the eye and challenge the enthusiastic amateur to try and identify. Many are endemics and not always easy to find in the standard flower books, although there are several available now which are very useful. A particularly beautiful book, although not one for the rucksack, is *Plantas do Algarve* published in 1991 with text in English and Portuguese. It has been specially written by the botanist Maria da Luz da Rocha Afonso to accompany sets of colour plates painted by the Scottish water-colourist, Mary McMurtrie. The plates have been arranged according to areas and habitat and so it is especially useful to the amateur. There is a very useful check-list of plants in the book by Wuerpel. Although this is out of print, copies are to be found in libraries and second-hand bookshops and it is worth looking for. Wuerpel's list is arranged according to geological area and the same order will be used here. Now another excellent book has been published, *Algarve plants and landscape*, by D.P.Mabberley and P.J.Placito. The illustrations in this book include ten species of orchid which are to be found in the Algarve.

SHALE ZONE

There are fewer species in this zone than any of the other areas. The most abundant is the gum cistus, *Cistus ladanifer*, which has large white flowers with a magenta splash on the base of each petal. The leaves are dark green and sticky and the plant often grows to a height of 2m or more. Vivid splashes of deep pink and white are provided by various tree heathers which flower most of the winter. The roadsides are often planted with acacias such as *Acacia dealbata* and *Acacia pycnantha* with their striking yellow scented flowers also brightening the landscape in winter. These are seen on the way up to Monchique from Portimão for example. There are groves of cork oaks, new plantations of eucalyptus and by streams there are always alders and stands of the giant reeds, *Arundo donax*. Oleanders with red and white flowers are also conspicuous on the banks of streams. *Arbutus unedo*, the strawberry tree, grows everywhere and in winter can be seen bearing both pale flowers and the fruits which are orange at first, darkening to a deep red when fully ripe. In spite of their reputation for being either tasteless or unpleasant, the ripe fruits are quite edible and thirst-quenching. They are used to make a liqueur, *medronho*, which is not particularly pleasant but is very strong.

Among the smaller plants are two types of lavender, purple *Lavandula stoechas* and green *Lavandula viridas*, wild gladiolus, wild nasturtiums and violets. In the east of the Algarve near the Rio Guadiana there are whole fields of white wild chamomile, scattered among which are some tiny purple irises, seen on Walk 23 near Azinhal. An endemic plant in the shales and seen also in sandy places near the coast is the Portuguese milk-vetch, a perennial herb growing up to 1m high. It blooms from January to May and has large creamy flowers in erect spikes and narrow lanceolate leaflets. It is poisonous to sheep and cattle. The tiny hoop-skirted narcisssus, *N. bulbocodium*, is found growing in large colonies on some of the shale cliffs in winter, as on the Praia do Castelejo cliffs, Walk 28.

SYENITE ZONE (SERRA DE MONCHIQUE)

The landscape here is dominated by trees. There are cork oaks, olives, pines and now the new plantations of eucalyptus. Groves of sweet chestnuts are seen here and there as on Walk 1 to Madrinha. Camellias flower in April and May. Tree heathers grow on Fóia (Walk 2) where in May large bushes of Rhododendron *ponticum sp.*

baeticum are a riot of purple flowers. This species only grows in the Iberian peninsula. The two lavenders grow in this area, foxgloves and primroses are found in damp places, there are stonecrops, crimson clover, early purple orchids, the wild western peony and many more. We found the tiny squill, *Scylla broteri*, growing in the woods near Alferce, but failed to find *Euphorbia moniquensis*, an endemic which only grows high up on Picota.

LIMESTONE

(a) The Barrocal. This hilly area is characterised by an association of plants often found in limestone areas. It includes mastic and turpentine bushes, rosemary, lavender, dwarf fan palms, grey-leaved cistus, asphodels and wild asparagus among others. Wild olives and carobs are among the trees. This association is well seen on Walk 15, Rocha de Pena. The rosemary growing in this area is unusual in being a decided lilac colour, in fact almost pink. Smaller flowers growing among the rock outcrops and boulders included the paper-white narcissus, *N. papyraceus*, and a tiny miniature daffodil, *N. gaditanus*. Another walk on a limestone hill, Cabeça Gorda (Walk 18), provided several flowers we had not seen before, such as a golden yellow anemome, *A. palmata* and a wild tulip with a lovely orange flower. The species growing in this area are too numerous to mention.

(b) The Plantation area. This area is characterised by the thousands of almond trees. Other trees include olives, carobs, figs, walnuts and nysperas or loquats. Along the road verges are pepper trees, cypresses, oleanders, Judas trees, pelargoniums and white and purple irises. The wild flowers are even more numerous in this zone and again too numerous to list. Among the most colourful are the ubiquitous Bermuda buttercup which makes beautiful golden carpets beneath the almond trees but is a serious weed as far as the horticulturalist is concerned. Field daisies, crown daisies, marguerites, vetch, field gladiolus, aromatic inula, wild honeysuckle, common mallow, lavender... the list is endless.

LOWER ZONE

There is an even greater variety of plants in this zone because there is more water and a diversity of habitats including the salt-marshes.

(See Ria Formosa Nature Park.) One striking plant is the imported but naturalised *Agave americana* or century plant. This has very sharp leaf edges so makes a good barrier. It throws up a tall mast-like flower spike after ten years and then dies, but leaves a group of new plantlets at its base. We have seen this used as a boundary or hedging plant near Pontal on Walk 27. White broom flowering in February is very pretty, blooming on roadside verges and even on the cliffs near Albufeira. Hottentot figs make carpets of red and yellow along the coastal areas. Many herbs grow wild along the cliff tops and by roadsides and edges of fields. These include thyme and fennel and several varieties of mint.

THE SAGRES PENINSULA AND THE WEST COAST

A limestone pavement area tops the cliffs of Cape St Vincent. To the north this gives way to shales and further north still there is the unique Pontal peninsula topped by massive sand dunes. Many endemic plants grow in this area which merits a separate description. The cliff-tops are windswept almost all the year round, and many plants grow in prostrate forms. Rosemary and even the acacias are ground-hugging. In spite of the wind there is an amazing variety of species making a colourful display throughout the spring, which begins quite early in the year.

One of the endemics is a dwarf form of *Cistus ladanifer*, ssp. *sulcatus*, formerly known as *Cistus palinhae* or Sagres gum cistus. This has shiny, sticky dark green leaves and white crinkly unblotched

flowers. Another is a thrift, *Armeria pungens*, which produces very tall pink flowerheads in March or even earlier. The milk vetch *Astralagus massiliensis* is one of the plants well equipped to deal with the dry conditions in having very spiky leaves, the plants forming gigantic 'pin-cushions' covered with pure white flowers. There are yellow rock-roses, blue pimpernels and deep red wild antirrhinums. The coastal walks are recommended to anyone with an interest in wild flowers, especially 24 to 30.

Portuguese milk-vetch

BIRDS, WILDLIFE AND PROTECTED AREAS

The variety of habitats in the Algarve, the agreeable climate and its position at the south-western corner of Europe all combine to make the area one that is rich in birdlife. Over 200 species of bird inhabit the area or pass through it during the spring and autumn migrations. Dedicated bird-watchers visit during these times, keeping watch on the sea-cliffs at Cape St Vincent to observe the passage of gannets, skuas, terns, shearwaters and other sea-birds. One report mentions a count of 6000 gannets during a 75 minute period on a day in mid-October. For the interested walker, many sea-birds are resident and can readily be seen at some of the sites described below.

Away from the coast and especially in the northern hills one bird likely to catch the eye of walkers is the azure-winged magpie with its bright blue wings and long blue tail. On many hill walks, especially near forests, woodpeckers are frequently heard calling but not so often seen. There are three species: green, greater-spotted and lesser-spotted. The wooded hills are also good for crested tits.

Areas of tangled scrubland make an ideal habitat for small songbirds which seem to delight in hiding themselves before they can be identified. Sardinian warblers are everywhere, stonechats are often seen perched on top of a long stalk and flocks of goldfinches are a frequent sight. Black redstarts are common and so are chiffchaffs, meadow pipits, robins and blackbirds. Crag martins are abundant near the coast as are shags, cormorants and many species of gull.

Exotic birds that are especially interesting are the storks which nest on town chimneys as well as tree tops, the large colonies of flamingoes and the avocets. All of these are easily seen. More rare was the purple gallinule we

Greater flamingo

25

saw at Ludo, a large bird with purple-blue plumage and red legs and feet. It was using its red bill to pull at the base of some reeds for food.

Walkers like myself who enjoy observing birds during the course of a walk and who want to recognise more birds cannot do better than to visit one or more of the Reserves in company with an expert such as John Measures who lives at Burgau. (See Useful Information.)

FAUNA

Although it is the bird population that is predominant in the Algarve there are a number of wild animals that should be mentioned. Still in existence but very rare are the wolf and the badger. The fox is becoming rare too but we certainly noticed the distinctive smell of fox on several walks. Less rare is the ring-tailed civet cat, which preys on poultry. Rabbits are more common than hares but both are hunted for sport and food. There is quite a large population of Egyptian mongoose, but they are nocturnal and not often seen. If you catch a fleeting glimpse of a furry animal rather like a cat or fox and it has a long tail with a bushy tuft at the end, it is a mongoose. There are several varieties of non-poisonous snake, the European green lizard, chameleons, geckos and salamanders. Some 300 species of butterfly are found in the Ria Formosa area and a leaflet on them is available from tourist offices.

NATURE RESERVES AND PROTECTED SITES

There are only two Nature Reserves in the Algarve: Ria Formosa and Castro Marim. Proposals are still being discussed to give protection to other areas such as Monchique, Rocha de Pena and the Alvor Estuary. Monchique is covered in Walks 1 to 3 and Rocha de Pena in Walks 14 and 15. The coastal sites are described below from west to east.

CAPE ST VINCENT

In spite of the massive tourist development of recent years the Algarve still has some beautiful and unspoilt areas. Outstanding among them is the west coast facing the Atlantic north of Cape St Vincent, already mentioned above. Since 1988 this has been a protected area so the outstanding cliff scenery and unique flora

Birdwatching at Alvor

should be safe for future generations to enjoy. See Walks 24 to 30 for further details.

ALVOR ESTUARY

This area is a peninsula between the Odiaxere stream and the Alvor river. There are several disused salinas and an area of marshland separated from the river by an embankment. On the low hill between the two is open scrubland and a few pine trees. The sandy bay is sheltered by sand banks and almost enclosed by them. On a visit there with John Measures we saw over 30 species of bird including Caspian terns, a whimbrel, turnstones, a kingfisher and a bluethroat.

The estuary is reached from the west by turning right at the crossroads for Mexilhoeira Grande. This is a very narrow lane immediately at the side of the garden centre. Drive down the lane to the end and park near an old abandoned bus. A short circular walk round the salina can be followed by a walk in the opposite direction to the river embankment. At low tide it is possible to walk along the sand. Anyone without a car could easily reach here by taking the train from Lagos to Mexilhoeira and walking down the

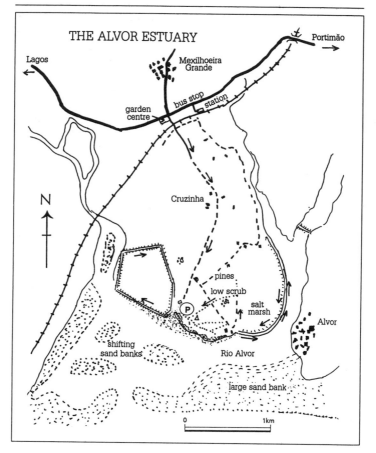

THE ALVOR ESTUARY

lane. There is a religious/ornithological station called La Rocha, at Cruzinho, on this lane which is open to visiting bird-watchers on Thursday afternoons or at other times by previous arrangement.

RIA FORMOSA NATURE PARK

The status of Ria Formosa dates from 1988. It is recognised as one of Europe's most important wetland areas and as a Nature Park is now

Black-winged stilt

protected from further exploitation and development. The approach to the airport gives a bird's eye view of this large wetland area which occupies 42,000 acres (17,000 hectares) and extends for 55km along the coast eastwards from Faro. It consists of a large lagoon in an advanced state of infilling, protected from the Atlantic by a necklace of sandspits and islands.

The interior of the lagoon is a salt-marsh through which run channels of brackish water. At high tides there is complete inundation and at low tides flat islands of rather uniform vegetation are exposed. Traditionally regarded as unhealthy and a breeding ground for mosquitoes, large areas have been drained, desalinated and reclaimed for agriculture. Now it is recogised that what is gained in this way is nothing compared with what is lost in terms of scientific, educative and even economic values. Rich in nutrients, the waters of the marsh support a food-chain culminating with many fish, shellfish and crustaceans which have been of great value to man over thousands of years.

The marsh vegetation is amazingly adapted to cope with the high salinity and the changing water levels. One of the first plants to colonise newly formed mud banks is spartina grass which can withstand long periods of inundation. When this is fixed, the current is slowed down, more sediments are trapped and other species begin to colonise. Mostly these are somewhat monotonous in appearance, but some of the higher plants add touches of colour, such as *Limoniastrum monopetalum* which forms dense bushes with lilac-pink flowers. There are interesting endemic

Avocet

29

species too such as *Cistanche phelipaea*, or salt-marsh broomrape which is a parasitic plant with striking yellow flower spikes.

The marshes are particularly important too as a haven for birds. These include avocets, ruffs, little egrets, black-tailed godwits and black-winged stilts. Grey, purple and night herons are fairly common. So are oystercatchers, not to mention coots, moorhens, mallard, shovelers and teal.

The sandspits and islands protecting the inner lagoon are different altogether from the marshes. The long sandspit of Ancoa in the west merges with the Ilha de Faro which can be reached by a causeway to the east of the airport. Separated from one another by narrow channels there are the islands of Barreta, Culatra, Armona, Tavira and Cabanas, the last one being almost connected to the sandspit of Manta Rota at the eastern end of the reserve. Culatra is inhabited and is reached by a 45 minute ferry ride from Olhão. Armona can be reached in 15 minutes from Olhão and the eastern end can be reached from Tavira by a bus which leaves the Praca da Republica to connect with the ferry. Access to the Ilha do Cabanas is from the town of Cabanas. These islands are very narrow; Ancoa is 9km by 150m, Tavira 11km by 500m. This means that the dune development is limited to a foredune only in most areas. The dunes are unstable, sand drying out at low tide and being blown to the back of the beach.

The vegetation in such conditions has a precarious existence. There are some very attractive and rare plants on these dunes and in the past overgrazing by animals and careless trampling by humans as well as extraction of sand for building has put some species in danger of extinction. More than that, destruction of the vegetation can pave the way for the levelling of the dunes by wind and sea so that the whole system is put at risk.

Plants growing on the dunes are in distinct zones. The first zone at the strandline on the seaward size includes sea rocket, prickly saltwort, sand sea couch, sea spurge and purple spurge. Further inland and higher up marram grass appears, one of the species whose roots are valuable in stabilising the dune. More diverse species grow near the top of the dune: sea bindweed, sea holly, sea crosswort, everlasting flowers, thyme, thrift, toadflaxes and catch-fly to mention a few. There is an interesting endemic plant, *Thymus carnosus*, in the form of a dark-green cushion plant, which releases a lavender-like scent when crushed. Other plants grow in the fixed sands behind the foredune. These include the beautiful blue flowers of the pimpernel *Anagallis monelli*.

The park covers a huge area but inland it is quite densely populated and access is limited to a number of key sites:

1. Quinta do Ludo:

The most westerly is near Faro airport at Quinta du Ludo. Recently walkways have been established and marked by posts with painted tops. It is intended to increase the number of these and possibly to link them in a series.

2. Ludo Marsh:

Nearer the airport is the Ludo Marsh itself, reached by turning right from the road to the airport on a road signposted Pontal. Permits are required to visit this area from the park office in Faro: Rua Teofilo Broga, 15-1, 8000 Faro (089) 27514.

3. Quinta Marim:

This is the showplace of the park with a new information centre in a carefully managed and restored area. It is 1.5km east of Olhão and reached by turning south towards the campsite on a corner by a petrol station. Cross the railway and the centre is found on the left of the track. Even if the centre itself is closed as on public holidays, the gates are not locked. There is a parking area and a picnic site near the centre itself. Within the reserve is a restored tidal mill, some Roman fish tanks, a bird-of-prey rehabilitation centre, a desertification study project and a centre for the breeding of the almost extinct Algarvian water dog. These dogs are unique in having webbed feet and were used by fishermen to help in landing catches and so on. Among the long list of birds we saw here were black-tailed godwit, little stint, ringed plovers, whimbrels, a kingfisher and a waxbill.

4. Tavira:

The public road to the ferry terminal is a good place for seeing many birds in the old salinas. Avocets, black-winged stilts, godwits, a little stint and three ruffs were among those we saw in a short visit.

CASTRO MARIM NATURE RESERVE

This reserve, created in 1976, lies between the towns of Castro

Marim and Vila real de São Antonio. It is bounded by the Rio Guadiana to the east and the roads EN125 and 125.6 to the west and occupies over 2000 hectares. The reserve is protected from hunting, fishing and commercial exploitation, although the *salinas* which comprise most of the area are still worked. These saltpans are of great importance because of their attraction for wading birds and are the reason for the creation of the reserve. One of the greatest attractions is the resident flock of flamingoes which can always be seen at some point in the area. Another intriguing sight is the storks nesting in the olive trees on the farmland which borders the reserve on the north. Black-winged stilts are also present in some numbers and will certainly be seen, along with grey herons, little terns, dunlins and hundreds of coot. Avocets are there, but not so easy to see.

At the time of writing the reserve has no entrance notice, no footpath signs and no hides, but it is early days and in time these may be provided. The entrance is found on the EN122, 1.2km north of the railway crossing and about 2km south of the centre of Castro Marim. Some information is available from an office within the castle of Castro Marim, but the opening times are uncertain and unless you come by car it is probably not worth going there. Arriving by train at Vila Real it is worth taking a taxi to the entrance gate to avoid walking along the main road. A car can be parked about 150m from the entrance gate by a ruined building.

It is possible to walk all round the track which encircles the saltpans. At one point it is necessary to go through an open gate with a 'no entry' sign near the saltworks. The track winds on and eventually reaches a pumping station at the most southerly point. From here an earthen embankment covered with Burmuda buttercups is followed, with the river on the right-hand side. The railway is seen on the other bank, but there is no way across except by completing the circuit and returning to the starting point. If you are travelling by train it is essential to allow plenty of time for this and 4 hours is suggested for full enjoyment of the reserve. Never attempt to take short cuts across the salina dykes as there are many gaps which are impossible to cross. If short of time, it is better to penetrate the reserve for a short distance only and return the same way.

Descending north side of Fóia. (Walk 2)

Pedralva *(Walk 7)*
Threshing floor on ridge *(Walk 8)*

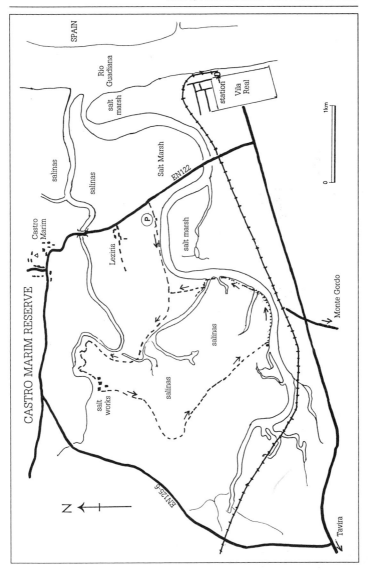

FORESTRY, AGRICULTURE AND
THE LANDSCAPE

In the shale areas in the north of the Algarve the predominant rural activity is forestry. There is an abrupt contrast between the steep-sided hills with their natural cover of gum cistus interspersed with arbutus trees and the hills which have been terraced and planted with trees. Here the bare reddish-brown earth is conspicuous in the young plantations and has its attractions, but the terracing itself looks ugly and unnatural. The population in these hills is low, but there are numerous isolated small farms and hamlets where a few fields grow vegetables and cereals. Sheep and goats are kept and taken out for grazing under the watchful eyes of one of the old people.

CORK

The evergreen oak, *Quercus suber*, is very important in the economy of Portugal which supplies over half the world's cork. Cork is a unique natural material, being strong, flexible and compressible. Apart from its use from time immemorial as a flask and bottle stopper, it provides floor and wall coverings, lifebelts, fishing floats and a hundred other items. It has even been used to line a space shuttle. Although the main area of production is the Alentejo, many oaks are also grown in the northern Algarve, both in the Serra de Monchique and in the shales of the Serra de Caldeiro. The foliage has a gold tinge in winter, but the trees are most recognisable by the bark which is pale grey and spongy when the trees are ready for stripping. When newly stripped the underlying trunk is a brilliant orange, which changes with time to a dark orange, then reddish brown, then brown, eventually darkening to grey-black and finally fading to pale grey.

Stripping takes place in midsummer, when the bark shrinks inwards away from the trunk. Skilled workers use a razor-sharp tool to make horizontal incisions first right round the tree and then link these with vertical cuts. The bark is then carefully removed without damaging the trunk beneath. The last two digits of the year

Cork oak

are then painted on in white paint, so '89' or '91' indicate the trees were last stripped in 1989 or 1991. Trees are not normally stripped all at once, but every three years or so some part of it will be stripped; either the lower part of the main trunk, or the upper part, or the large limbs. The trees take about twenty-five years to mature and are then stripped every nine or ten years until after 150 to 170 years the quality falls off and they are abandoned.

After stripping the sections of bark are piled up for initial curing, then taken to cork collection points. From here they are taken to factories and boiled in water for several hours to make them flexible, then flattened and stored until required. Trees at all stages will be observed during the walks and in some cases the paths made by the cork strippers from one tree to another will be followed.

EUCALYPTUS

The planting of this fast-maturing species to provide pulp for the paper industry is a controversial matter. The economic advantages are obvious and Portugal needs the income, but local farmers and environmentalists are concerned about the effects on the water-table, the increased fire risk and the depletion of soil nutrients. Although by 1990 more than 15% of Portugal's forests were planted with eucalyptus, recent plantings have included more pine.

The species most often planted is *E. globulus ssp. globulus* which has single flowers. There are eucalyptus plantations in the syenite area of Monchique also, seen on Walks 2 (Fóia) and 3 (Picota). The seedlings are planted densely and coppiced after eight years. Regrowth is fast and after thinning the new shoots are left for another eight years and coppiced again. After about thirty years the trees are replanted. All the forest litter is left where it falls and this smothers growth of other species and gives a rather untidy look to some of the tracks.

In the Algarve eucalyptus timber is also used in the building industry for scaffolding poles and for beams and roof trusses and for construction of the plastic-covered greenhouses known as *estufas*.

PINE

Pine is grown in coastal areas as well as in the hills for both timber and turpentine. Both *Pinus pinaster* and *Pinus pinea* are used in shipbuilding and for constructing the mule carts still used in the countryside today. *Pinus pinea*, the stone pine, or Umrella pine, is also grown for the pine nuts especially near the coast. The stands make attractive shady places. The cones are knocked down by canes of *Arundo donax* when they ripen in February. Extracting the nuts is laborious which is why the nuts are expensive.

CHESTNUT

This is not a native tree but has been grown in the Monchique area for many years, mainly for furniture making. Hand-crafted 'Monchique chairs' with rush fibre seats and backs and with painted decorations may be seen displayed in the town. Stands of chestnut will be seen on Walk 2, Fóia.

CHARCOAL

Charcoal is still produced in some quantity and is used mainly for cooking fish on open grills and barbecues. Even in towns local people may be seen cooking fish for their lunch on one of these grills just outside the front door. The charcoal is produced by the slow burning of a mound of wood for about ten days, the correct rate of burning being maintained by drilling airholes through the pile as necessary. Large sheets of bark on the surface of the heap prevent too much air getting in. Although most of this charcoal is produced in the northern area, we have seen charcoal burners at work in almond orchards of the Barrocal. It seems a good use for accumulated piles of prunings.

Charcoal making near Paderne

TRADITIONAL FRUIT TREES

Small farming is the normal practice in the Algarve, unlike the Alentejo to the north where there are vast flat plains all growing cereals and cork oaks. These small farms, mainly in the Barrocal limestone area and in the eastern littoral, all grow various combinations of Mediterranean fruit trees with an underplanting of cereals or grass for grazing animals and small fields of peas and beans. The trees chosen are those that once established require little or no watering and are easy to look after: figs, olives, carobs, almonds and vines.

Figs were formerly very important in the rural economy and many tons were exported. Now many of the trees are neglected but they are still a feature of the winter landscape with pale grey bare branches that upturn at the ends. One reason for the decline is that land has been sold to developers, especially in the region around Albufeira. Production of olives and olive oil is also declining, despite its importance in the local economy for the same reason. The silvery grey of the evergreen foliage is always a delight to the eye, as are the gnarled and twisted forms of the old trees which can live to a thousand years and more. October walkers will see olives being harvested by knocking them off with long canes or poles. We did see evidence in some areas that olive production might be on the increase, in the form of newly grafted trees, for example in Walk 9, Pico Alto. Carobs, like olives, are also evergreen and the new growth each year is a lighter, brighter green than the old giving a pleasing variegated appearance. The fruits are long pods which turn black when ripened in the sun. They are used as animal fodder as well as to produce a gum used in foodstuffs and carob flour for a healthier alternative to chocolate.

The flowering of the almond trees in January and February is one of the great sights of the Algarve. Rogue trees may be found in flower in early December. Different cultivars flower at different times so that some trees may be seen in flower as late as March. Like olives, almonds are harvested by knocking them off the trees with long poles. This takes place at the end of August. They are an important commercial product, but production has suffered from encroachment of the tourist industry, especially in the Albufeira area. A by-product of the industry is the use of the husks in firing pottery kilns, but enormous heaps of discarded husks are often noticed in the countryside.

Small vineyards are seen on many walks, both in the Barrocal and in the coastal areas. The grapes are sold for eating in the local markets and also used for winemaking. There are wine co-operatives in Lagoa, Tavira, Portimão and Lagos which produce about 80% of all the Algarvian wine from some 300 small vineyards. Most of the wine is consumed locally although a little is exported, some to the UK.

OTHER CROPS

Maize and winter cereals such as wheat and oats are grown on many small farms. Winnowing is carried out on the spot and threshing floors are a feature seen on many walks. They vary enormously in size and may be floored by beaten earth, bricks, tiles or concrete. Corn kernels were seen drying in the sun at Esteveira, the discarded husks nearby. Rice is still produced near Aljezur and was formerly grown near Silves. Peas and beans are commonly planted in small fields near farmhouses or below almonds or carobs. Because of the mild climate, three or even four crops a year may be grown and

Corn drying near Rogill

delicious new ones appear in the markets in February. Broad beans or *favas* are a favourite with both *Algarvios* and visitors as either an accompanying vegetable or the basis of a main dish. Dried and salted ones are sold as an enjoyable snack-food, but beware the ones that are *piripiri* flavoured. The *hortas* or market gardens grow almost every kind of vegetable known to man and they are all on sale virtually all the year round making a colourful display in the markets.

CITRUS FRUITS

Unlike the traditional trees already mentioned, citrus require irrigation during the dry summer months. Always grown in areas with the highest rainfall, the construction of new reservoirs has enabled many new plantations to be made on the coastal plains, although not too near the sea as they are not salt-tolerant. The trees flower from March to May, filling the air with their heady perfume and the fruits ripen from October onwards and in January and February are available in abundance. One of the delights of a winter holiday is buying several kilos of oranges very cheaply and drinking unlimited amounts of freshly squeezed orange juice. Besides the sweet oranges, which are the most important, there are tangerines, mandarins, clementines and satsumas. Lemons and limes are also grown, but grapefruit is rare.

OTHER FRUITS

Apples, pears, peaches and apricots are grown. Of the soft fruits, only strawberries are significant. Winter holidaymakers will find them in the markets from the end of January onwards. One fruit unfamiliar to many British visitors is the loquat or nyspera, the Japanese medlar. The trees are quite striking, being upright and with large shiny evergreen leaves with prominent veins. The flowers appear in late autumn and the yellow fruits mature in late spring. We noticed many of these trees on the Ilha do Rosário, Walk 6, and near the Fonte de Benémola, Walk 16.

EXOTIC CROPS AND SALADS

Bananas and papayas are grown outdoors in favoured spots and in the enormous polythene greenhouses that dominate the landscape

Old cork beehives near Espargal

near Faro. These *estufas* are mainly used for year-round production of salad vegetables and tomatoes. In February we saw lettuces growing outside without any protection near Pico Alto, Walk 9. On another occasion while exploring for a walk we came across watercress being grown on narrow north-facing terraces in the Monchique area. In the early morning a thin sheet of ice had formed on the surface of the gently running water, yet at midday higher up the sun was as hot as usual.

BEEKEEPING

Honey is produced almost everywhere in the Algarve and rows of beehives are a common sight on many walks. In the high *serra* the bees forage among the eucalyptus, heathers, strawberry trees and acacias as well as the gum cistus; in the Barrocal on a greater variety of plants. Nowadays most beehives are of planks, but several times we have come across some made in the traditional way from curved sheets of cork. Locally produced honey may be found on sale in the markets, but the honey on the supermarket shelves is mainly from Australia.

Old well near river Algibre

IRRIGATION AND WATER SUPPLIES

In the interior of the Algarve, wherever the land is cultivated, many wells will be noticed. Almost every house and smallholding has its own. The deep circular wells known as *noras* were formerly operated by a blindfolded mule harnessed to a metal arm which pulled up a long chain of buckets. Another type are known as *cegonhas*, or storks, from the shape of the long counterbalanced beam with a hanging pole to which a bucket is attached which looks like the long beak of a stork. These are used in the dry season of late autumn to raise the water flowing several feet below the dry stream-beds. Many are now abandoned, the lifting machinery being replaced by electric pumps. This water is strictly for the irrigation of vegetable crops.

For drinking water, deep boreholes must be drilled, sometimes several hundred feet deep. In some remote places people must fetch water from springs, using a mule to carry the water in large earthenware jars. Even in Faro, a water cart selling fresh water was in use until 1974. This cart is preserved and can be seen in the Ethnographic Museum in the town.

Houses in many villages are still dependent on a communal water supply. For some, a village washplace is a recent innovation. These new installations have a small *cisterna* nearby, filled by a hand-wheel operated pump. The water is then gravity fed to the washplace through a pipe with a tap. Sloping scrubbing boards are often built on round the sides. In other villages, women can still be seen washing clothes in the river or carrying the laundry to or from the river in a load balanced on their heads.

In 1991 and 1992 there was a serious water shortage in the Algarve. Several dry summers caused problems as more and more water was consumed in ever increasing tourist accommodation. New golf courses requiring millions of gallons every day for watering the greens add to the problem. Afforestation with eucalyptus which requires enormous quantities of water does nothing to help. Although large dams are being constructed, like the Barragem do Silves across the Arade river, they are hardly keeping pace with the increased consumption. A higher rainfall in 1993 seems to have eased the problem, but some long-term solution is needed as one bad season with water rationing or no water at all could ruin the tourist trade on which the economy depends almost completely.

PLANTS USED IN COTTAGE INDUSTRIES

The giant reeds, *Arundo donax*, are used to make fishing rods and walking sticks. They are harvested annually and are often seen stacked upright against a wall to dry in the sun. Another traditional use for these is as a support for roofing tiles, seen in both old and modern buildings.

Baskets have always been needed to collect, transport and store the fruit harvest, so they have always been made from whatever plants were available locally. These include willow, wattle, rush, esparto grass and even fennel stalks. The dwarf fan palm is particularly favoured and used for all kinds of bags, mats, hampers and even hats as well as baskets. Originally only made for local use, some of these products may be found on sale at the *Artesenatos* or hand-craft shops all over the Algarve.

HISTORICAL PERSPECTIVE

There is evidence that the Algarve was inhabited by early man, certainly in the area around Silves where neolithic axes, adzes and chisels have been found. At Alcalar to the north of Portimão there is a megalithic grave or tumulus. It is a sunken circular chamber and corridor, dated at 2000-600 BC. Although it has not been fully restored, some work was being done to drain and conserve it in November 1993. With its agreeable climate and fertile soil it was probably a settlement of some importance before the Romans appeared on the scene about 218 BC. The most lasting mark made on the landscape by the Romans, who occupied the area for some 600 years, was the road system, the routes of which are still in use today. The Romans built towns and bridges, improved castles and defences and started small industries such as fish-salting stations. Some of these Roman fish-tanks have been restored at Quinta Marim, the newly opened visitor centre for the Ria Formosa Nature Park. A Roman bridge is crossed near Paderne in Walk No. 10.

It may be that the Romans introduced the principles of irrigation, but it was the North African Moors who invaded the Iberian peninsula in AD711 who had the greatest influence on the landscape and who were responsible for the wells, the waterwheels and the agricultural system. The Moors gave the Algarve its name, 'Al Gharb' meaning western land, and the style of building still in use today, with low white buildings and rounded arches, the blue and white tiles or *azulejos* and the highly decorative filigree chimney-pots. The Moorish capital was Silves, then known as Chelb. It was an important and civilised town and trading area with direct access to the sea by the Arade river. The population in its heyday was well over 30,000 and it was said to be like Baghdad with mosques, bazaars and many citrus orchards. Now the river is silted up and not navigable, but there is still a huge monthly market held on the flat fields beside the river. When Silves fell in 1189 to a combined attack from the King of Portugal, Dom Sancho I, and crusaders from England and Germany, it was the beginning of the end of Moorish domination.

In 1249 King Alfonso II of Portugal finally brought the rule of the

Moors to an end and subsequent rulers were always known as 'Kings of Portugal and the Algarve', an acknowledgement of the separate identity of the Algarve. (This practice continued until the overthrow of the monarchy in 1910.) In subsequent years there were many disputes and challenges from Castile which must be omitted from this short account. One event worth mentioning though is the marriage of King Jão I to Philippa, the daughter of John O'Gaunt, from which began the long alliance of Portugal with England. In the fifteenth century it was their son Henry 'The Navigator' who instigated and sponsored the great voyages of exploration which were made from the Algarvian ports of Sagres and Lagos. Madeira and the Azores were discovered, and gradually the western coast of Africa was followed further and further south, culminating, after Henry's death, with the rounding of the Cape of Good Hope by Bartolomeu Dias in 1488 and Vasco da Gama's voyage to Calcutta in 1498.

From the fifteenth to the twentieth centuries the fortunes of the Algarve continued to be bound up with the attempts at domination by Spain, leading to bizarre events (in terms of Portuguese and British friendship) such as the attack on Lagos and Sagres in 1587 by Sir Francis Drake and the sacking of Faro in 1596 by the Earl of Essex. The bishop's library in Faro was stolen and presented to the Bodleian in Oxford.

One catastrophic event in this period was the 1755 earthquake during which almost all the buildings in Lisbon, the Alentejo and the Algarve were destroyed. A tidal wave 20m high deposited sand in harbours and river-mouths. Minor earthquakes are fairly common with over 1000 being recorded in a period of 200 years.

In 1807 Portugal was invaded by Napoleon and during the Peninsular war British and Portuguese troops under the command of Wellington drove the French out of Portugal. In 1910 the monarchy was ended and a Republic proclaimed. A period of turmoil followed, with great economic difficulties. By 1928 control fell into the hands of Salazar, first of all as Minister of Finance and then as Prime Minister, establishing a dictatorship parallel to that of Franco in Spain. This was a time of great poverty and no personal freedom and which continued until the 'Carnation' revolution of 1974.

THE REVOLUTION AND ITS BACKGROUND

Salazar became ill and died in 1970. He had been replaced by Caetano who was not a strong personality. Guerrilla warfare was increasing in Africa, illegal strikes were taking place in the mainland and political opposition was beginning to emerge. In February 1974 Spinola's book *Portugal and its future* was published, a book which had a great deal of influence. On April 25th a coup by MFA (the Armed Forces Movement) overthrew Caetano. This was an almost completely bloodless revolution in which soldiers carried carnations in the barrels of their rifles.

Things were not plain sailing after this. During the first moderate phase there were three provisional governments. In 1975 a more radical phase began and the fourth provisional government decreed large scale nationalisation of private monopolies. There was increasing land occupation in southern Portugal. Eventually the radical elements were so divided among themselves that increasingly conservative elements took over. In 1976 elections took place and constitutional government began. The principles of a pluralist democracy were established and people found themselves with greater political freedom than they had ever known.

Gum cistus

NOTES FOR WALKERS

GRADING OF WALKS

Most walks in the Algarve make use of old mule-tracks or cart-tracks which until recently were normally the only means of communication between villages. Underfoot the going varies from smooth earth tracks to rough and stony ones but is not usually pathless. Sometimes narrow trods used by men harvesting cork are followed; these tend to be overgrown by *matos*. In other places the bulldozers have been at work, widening old paths or linking terraces prepared for planting trees. Short cuts through *matos* are not recommended; it can be very dense and the gum cistus is exceptionally sticky. Most of the walks are not particularly strenuous, ascents of 500m being about the maximum. Each walk has been described either as very easy, easy, moderate, or difficult. The time given is for general guidance and represents an average person's pace with occasional pauses for photography and so on but does not include longer stops for rests or refreshments. Distances for many walks can only be approximate as so many paths and tracks are not on the published maps. Similarly figures for height gained are often an approximation and are not given unless this is an appreciable amount.

MAPS

The Algarve is covered by 14 sheets in the Carta Geografico do Portugal 1:50,000 series published by the Instituto Geografico e Cadastral. Unfortunately these were published about thirty years ago and so do not include the enormous changes that have occurred since then, especially in the last decade. Although most of the new developments have been in a narrow strip along the south coast the inland areas have also been affected, especially since Portugal joined the EEC. Money has suddenly become available and new roads are cutting across the countryside. These may or may not follow the course of old tracks and paths marked on the map. When using these maps to find a walk it can be disconcerting to find that a narrow and winding path has become a broad track with the bends smoothed out, or an old cart-track has been upgraded to a drivable road and in some cases surfaced. In other cases old paths have disappeared entirely from a combination of disuse and encroaching vegetation. Nevertheless the maps have their uses as long as these limitations are borne in mind. It is advisable to obtain the latest available road map to use in conjunction with the 1:50,000 sheets. Note that the sketch-maps in this book show only features necessary to follow the relevant walk.

Maps may be obtained from the office of the *Instituto* in Faro in the form of flat sheets at a cost of 650$00 each. The address is 18 Rue Francisco Barreto and this street is found opposite the east end of the railway station and at right-angles to the railway. Office hours are 10.00-12.00 and 14.00-16.00. Alternatively buy them before you go from:

> The Map Shop at 15 High Street, Upton-upon-Severn, Worcs WR8 0HJ. Cost is £4.30 (1992).
> Stanfords, 27A Floral Street, London WC2E 9LP

If in stock they are supplied in a few days but if they have to be ordered delivery is 4 to 5 weeks. The most useful maps for the walker are 49C, 49D and 50D. (See Maps of the Algarve.)

ACCESS

After the peaceful revolution of 1974 the large country estates of Portugal, mainly in the Alentejo but also in the northern Algarve, were divided up and distributed among the people. Boundaries were marked out by stoneposts with the initials of the owner and in some cases by cairns with painted white stones. It is as well for walkers to be aware that these cairns represent land boundaries and not to expect them to indicate a footpath as in many other countries. Fenced land is very rare, except in the case of orchards and market gardens, especially when these are near to towns and occasionally enclosing land where animals such as goats are being reared. In some areas of the Barrocal there are stone walls of great thickness, but this is a result of the land being cleared of stone for arboriculture rather than an attempt to keep people out; in one area walls 3m thick were observed.

During the course of exploring the walks for this book not once did we find any objection to our presence. In fact the opposite was the case and everyone we encountered in the countryside was friendly and welcoming. One day an elderly couple clearing weeds from their open fields of almonds and carobs came and sat with us as we ate lunch. Our very limited vocabulary of Portuguese and their complete lack of any English was no barrier to an enjoyable encounter and a lively conversation supported by sign-language. 'Private' notices are rare. They are more likely to be seen next to new villas belonging not to Portuguese but to incoming foreigners.

HAZARDS

Shooting

Although said to be on the decline, hunting is still a popular national pastime. In 1988 laws were passed regularising what had been a chaotic situation with uncontrolled and unlicensed shooting over vast areas and by large numbers of people. Since then those who want to hunt must apply for a licence and take a test for it too. Hunting zones are defined and hunting restricted to Thursdays, Sundays and feast days. Rabbits, hares, foxes and all kinds of bird including small songbirds like thrushes are all targeted and in fact small birds are regarded as a great delicacy for the pot. Marion Kaplan says that 'hunters still outnumber birdwatchers by a disheartening 3,000 to one'. Possibly this activity will decline thanks to increased environmental protection, the creation of more wildlife areas and the education of children in the appreciation of nature and the countryside without the wholesale slaughter of birds and beasts.

Meanwhile it is advisable for walkers to beware of wandering into a shooting party on a Sunday. Accidents can and do happen and it is not unknown for hunters to shoot each other or their own dogs. Near the village of Ribeira do Algibre while investigating a walk for this book we found ourselves among a large shooting party. Small groups of men and boys dressed up in camouflage clothing were stationed strategically behind bushes and rocks. Vast piles of empty cartridge cases littered the ground. None of us had seen the like before and when shot started whizzing past our ears at an uncomfortably close distance it seemed better to go on than to go back. Be warned: if sounds of heavy shooting are heard, choose another walk.

Various signs in red have lately (1993) been erected on various boundaries. Their meanings are all to do with hunting and have nothing to do with footpaths or rights of way. As far as I have been able to ascertain they mean:

'No hunting', 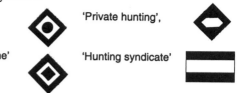 'Private hunting',

'Tourist hunting zone' 'Hunting syndicate'

Snares and traps

Although these are illegal some may still be found on paths in remote countryside. Two members of our walking party were caught by them. They do not do much damage but can be an unpleasant shock.

Bees

There are beehives everywhere and while bees do not normally attack people it is safer to give them a wide berth. The author was stung by a bee returning to the hives, while sitting on a flight path from a valley to the hives placed on a high ridge. Best treatment is to remove the sting immediately, preferably with tweezers. Anyone allergic to bee stings should take the appropriate medication with them.

Mosquitoes

Occasionally these may be a nuisance and it is worth taking insect repellant and also anti-histamines in case of an allergic reaction. These can be bought at chemists in the Algarve if necessary.

Dogs

Algarvian dogs are not normally a hazard. Most of them are small, friendly and very sociable. There are many of them and they can be very noisy and sometimes a nuisance, but we never saw a fierce one. On the contrary, one whose siesta we disturbed ran away as fast as possible after a token bark. Another dog followed us several miles, never being a nuisance in any way but apparently enjoying our company. As we intended catching a bus at a different point to where we started it was a relief when it turned back for home. Those who are frightened of dogs or who encounter one who appears to be vicious should do as the Portuguese do; pick up a stone and threaten to throw it. Imaginary stones often do the trick in the absence of the real thing.

River crossings
Throughout the year most streams are almost or completely dry. However, after winter rains these same streams can be swollen to an unimaginable degree. By one such crossing where we were able to cross dry-shod, water-borne debris was observed a good 3m above the normal low level. It is self-evident that walks which involve any river crossings cannot be attempted in these circumstances.

Car thefts
Police advise people never to leave valuables in their cars and to leave the cars locked.

Equipment and clothing
In the winter dress as for reasonable summer conditions in Britain. A light sweater is often necessary early in the morning and at the end of the day. A lightweight anorak or a waterproof is an insurance against the odd shower or in windy conditions. Lightweight boots are preferred at all times by the author but some walkers find trainers or walking shoes are adequate. Snow is almost unheard of and many young *Algarvios* have never seen it. When it rains, it rains, usually all day. Stay in and read a book, go shopping, visit a museum, or indulge in a special long lunch. Anyone walking in summer will require sun protection and water.

WALKER'S COUNTRY CODE

The importance of adhering to this code of practice for walking in the countryside cannot be over-emphasised. Although this is now well publicised in almost every guidebook and in articles in the 'outdoor press' it can do no harm to repeat these rules here:

1. Guard against risk of fire, especially in woodland and scrub.
2. Re-close and fasten all gates.
3. Keep dogs under control and on leads when near livestock.
4. Keep to paths on farmland and avoid growing crops.
5. Avoid damaging fences, hedges and walls.
6. Leave no litter.
7. Safeguard water supplies. There is an acute shortage of water in the Algarve.
8. Protect wildlife, plants and trees.
9. Go carefully on country roads. Horses and carts or donkeys are frequently encountered in the Algarve.
10. Respect the life and work of people in the countryside.

Western Iberian squill

MAPS OF THE ALGARVE

The Algarve is covered by 14 sheets of the 1:50,000 maps of Portugal produced by the Instituto Geografico e Cadastral. The three most useful ones for walkers are 49C, 49D and 50C.

	49A Odeciexe 1981	49B S. Marcos da Serra 1960	50A Ameixial 1961	50B Alcoutim 1965
48D Bordeira 1963	49C Monchique 1963	49D Silves 1964	50C S. Brás de Alportel 1984	50D Vila Real de San António 1964
51B Vila do Bispo 1963	52A Portimão 1963	52B Albufeira 1964	53A Faro 1964	53B Tavira 1981(1978)

1: MADRINHA FROM GRALHOS

The summit of Madrinha at 802m is one of the high points of the Serra de Monchique and provides extensive views. This walk includes an almost level track which contours for over 3km at a height of about 750m, with a good surface leaving one free to enjoy the fine views to the north-west. The return route passes through the small hamlet of Pé do Frio where white houses are scattered here and there on the steep terraced hillside. The route is partly on the Monchique granite and partly on acid shale which gives a different vegetation. Gum cistus, arbutus and tree heathers are conspicuous over the shales. Eucalyptus and pine grow in both areas and mimosa does exceptionally well on the granite. The endemic *Rhododendron ponticum ssp.baeticum* grows on the granite along with foxgloves and primroses.

The walking is mainly easy on good tracks with an ascent of about 400m. The descent track is rather stony at first, followed by easy walking on a fairly level unsurfaced road on the return. Distance: 13.5km. Time: About 4hrs. Map: 49C Monchique. Grade: Moderate.

To reach the starting point turn left towards Marmelete from the Portimão-Monchique road and at Gralhos turn right along the unsurfaced road signposted Chilrão 6. Park at the wide col reached in 500m.

There are two tracks on the right-hand side of the road facing in the Chilrão direction. Take the left-hand one of these, not the one with the gateposts. It is a pleasant earth track through eucalyptuses and pines at first and then through open ground giving views of cultivated terraces in between the trees. Further on it is laid with flat stones, the signs of a really old track. After about 15 minutes go

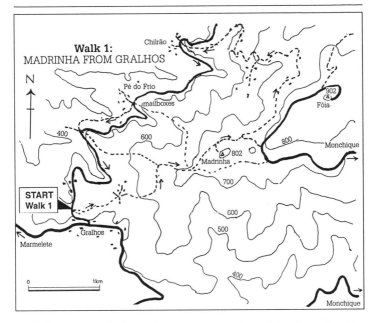

Walk 1:
MADRINHA FROM GRALHOS

N

Chilrão

Pé do Frio

mailboxes

400

600

902
Fóia

800

Monchique

Madrinha 802

700

START
Walk 1

600

Gralhos

500

Marmelete

400

0   1km

400

Monchique

straight on at a col where there are several branch tracks and paths both left and right. Keep on the main track ignoring a short cut left for the sake of better views and in a further 10 minutes take a branch track right at the side of a wood. Ignore a track left and after passing a field house follow the main track left into a wood where it levels out. When the track emerges from the trees the views suddenly open out ahead and another track is met at a T-junction. Turn right and the top of Madrinha with its fire-tower will be seen ahead. Follow the track up as it curves to the right and then back left towards the north side of Madrinha. Ignore a branch right by some trees, then cut across right to join the wide track which leads up to the top.

Return down the same way to re-join the main track and about 5 minutes later turn sharp left towards a large tree. Before reaching the tree a short cut can be taken on the right. Follow the level track along to the north-east, soon joining a more major track dropping down from the Fóia road. This continues to contour above old terraces and passes an inhabited house, before crossing a stream-bed where it turns sharp left into a wood.

Emerging from the wood the track passes a large stand of sweet chestnuts just before reaching a newly restored house. After this it begins to descend in wide bends, then makes a long detour north before swinging back to the south. Ignore minor branch tracks but at the first major junction bear right downhill and again right at the next major junction. After ignoring a diagonal cross-track and descending a litle further a wide unsurfaced road is met at a col. Turn left passing the signpost to Portelo do Viuva and the junction right into Chilrão. Keep on the wide track which contours to cross a stream before turning right and rising to reach the hamlet of Pé do Frio. At a cluster of mail boxes turn right on to an old narrow road which is more pleasant to walk on than the new. It goes below a small house and then contours before rising to meet the new road at a five-way junction on a col. Follow the new road back to the starting point.

2: FÓIA FROM MONCHIQUE

There cannot be another mountain top so disfigured as is the summit of Fóia. There is a positive forest of radio and television masts, a radar station surrounded by a rusty iron fence, a large obelisk and a complex of buildings with gift shops, restaurant and bar. As it can be reached by a motor road from Monchique many people drive there to enjoy the extensive views because at 902m Fóia is the highest point of the Algarve. It might be thought from this description that such a mountain top is best avoided, but my intentions are not to put people off walking there, rather to warn them what to expect. In fact the walk described is delightful and should not be missed. The horrors of the top are unseen most of the time.

The old town of Monchique where the walk begins and ends is very attractive, being built on a hillside with many steep and winding narrow streets. The ascent route goes through mixed woodland with areas of high altitude farming and a variety of crops grow on well-built terraces. Fóia is in the granite area of the Serra de Monchique and outcrops of this pale grey coarsely crystalline rock are seen in many places. There is an abundance of sage-leaved cistus flowering in early spring, with large white tree heathers flowering all winter. Later on there are the rhododendrons, with foxgloves and primroses in shady places. The drive up to Monchique from Portimão by car or bus is by a pleasant mountain road lined by mimosa trees making vivid splashes of bright yellow in January and February.

A fairly easy ascent mainly on good tracks and paths and with a climb of about 500m at a reasonable gradient. The descent is pathless at first and then on a stony eroded track before reaching easier ground. Distance: 11km. Time: 3hrs 20mins. Map: Monchique 49C. Grade: Moderate.

The first part of the ascent to the old convent of Nossa Senhora de Desterro is complicated but pictorial signs all the way make it easy to follow. From the main square in Monchique go up the narrow street at the side of the bus station. This is cobbled with shallow steps in the centre. Turn left almost immediately into the very narrow Travess das Guerreiras and go up the steps ahead which

Mimosa or silver wattle

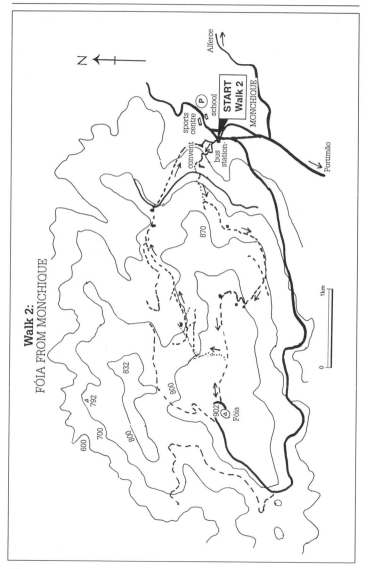

Walk 2:
FÓIA FROM MONCHIQUE

START
Walk 2

MONCHIQUE

Alferce

Portimão

school

P

sports centre

convent

bus station

870

832

792

700

600

800

800

902

Fóia

1km

0

curve right and then left. Cross a street and continue up fairly steeply to reach the ruined Colegio do Santa Caterina. Turn left in front of this and right a minute later. After another 2 minutes or so when the track bends right go straight on past a water pumping station on the left. Continue ascending to the old convent from which there are fine views over Monchique to Picota. At the time of writing the convent itself is ruinous and locked up. It takes about 15 minutes to reach this point and it is one of the steepest parts of the ascent.

Continue the walk by turning uphill into the woodland at the side of the convent, reaching an old path a couple of minutes later and turning left. When this bends sharp left keep straight on to reach an unsurfaced road at a bend. Turn left along this and after about 100m turn right onto an eroded but well-defined track slanting back right. After 2 minutes or a little less turn left and in another 4 minutes turn right at a T-junction on to a wider track. When another track is met at a bend turn left downhill and in a further 4 minutes join another track in a narrow valley opposite a water tank. Turn right, uphill this time, and follow the track as it curves into the stream bed and out again, passing a house hedged with the very spiky shrub *Asparagus stipularis*. The track begins to curve right and goes uphill into a side valley. Go straight on where a branch track doubles back right. Four minutes later ignore a track left as the main track swings uphill fairly steeply through a eucalyptus wood. Six minutes later keep straight on at a diagonal cross-track. The trees are then left behind and open ground covered with cistus shrubs is reached.

The summit masts are seen ahead for a short time, but disappear from view when the track swings right after passing a small house. At another house take the track which swings sharp right and at first descends slightly. It soon swings left again, crossing open ground and running parallel to the valley of Monchique. After rounding a corner the masts come into view again and are reached some 20-25 minutes later. On the right-hand side of the track is a valley with old cultivation terraces and a couple of deserted houses.

Before descending, it is worthwhile continuing past all the buildings for the sake of the views, especially on a clear day when the coastline to the west and south is visible. To descend, go back to the slight dip between the two sets of masts and start back down the track. After 5 minutes or so start descending into the first valley on rough ground, making towards a prominent outcrop of granite. At first there is no path but below the old grassy terraces a narrow trod can be picked up. This crosses the stream between high bushes of tree heather, rhododendrons and a tangle of brambles and bracken. A path on the other side goes down steeply then almost immediately re-crosses the stream. At this point there are still some of the original stone cobbles in place but most of them have been washed away leaving deep erosion channels.

Soon the track leaves the side of the stream-bed and descends more gradually on the right-hand side of the valley above a stand of sweet chestnuts. At a cross track turn left, following the main track downhill to join a more major track in the valley bottom. Turn right here and 2 minutes later ignore a branch track right leading uphill. Five minutes later join a more major track at a diagonal T-junction and turn right going slightly uphill at first. Half a minute later the track bends right through a cutting into a side valley and descends gently below green terraces on which cattle or sheep graze. Some 20 minutes later the track swings left by a small house. Take the short cut down an old cobbled path at the side of the house and go straight on down the continuation of this where it is cut by the new wide unsurfaced road. Views of Monchique and Picota open up. The cobbled track becomes steeper lower down and leads into an old part of the town. About 10 minutes later turn right at a T-junction opposite a small tavern with a tiled wall. After passing a blue and white tiled washplace turn right. Turn right at the T-junction at the bottom of the hill. When the main street is met turn right to reach the shallow steps leading back down to the main square by the bus station.

3: PICOTA FROM FORNALHA

This hill of 774m lies east of Monchique and is in the form of a north-east to south-west ridge, partly wooded but with granite outcrops. Unlike Fóia to the west whose summit is despoilt by a forest of masts and antennae, Picota has only a fire-watching tower beside the trig point. The views on a clear day are superb although restricted here and there by fast-growing eucalyptus trees. The approach from the

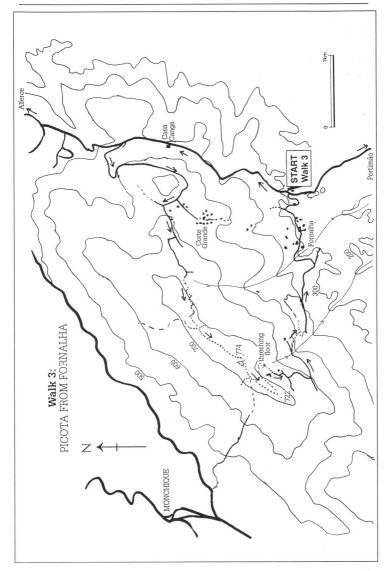

Walk 3:
PICOTA FROM FORNALHA

south-east side is very quiet and although partly on a surfaced road there is virtually no traffic. To reach the start, either drive to Alferce from Monchique and turn right to Fornalha at the entrance to the village, or turn right from the Portimão-Monchique road 3km north of Porto do Lagos. In either case park near the Fornalha turning which is signposted 'Telephone'.

Almost entirely on country roads and tracks with short stretches on good paths. A fairly gradual ascent of about 500m. Distance: 15km. Time: 4hrs 20min. Map: 49C Monchique. Grade: Moderate.

The walk begins with an uphill stretch of almost 3km along the road towards Alferce. Turn left up the narrow signposted road towards Corte Pequena through areas of mixed woodland interspersed with open ground. Ignore the left turn to Corte Grande and later ignore another left turn with an illegible signpost. The main road bends 90° right and uphill then turns sharp left at a col. When a cross-track is reached at a flattish area turn right and follow the track which soon dwindles to a narrow path heading westerly towards the Picota ridge. The path becomes slightly overgrown as the ridge is met. Turn left along the ridge and one minute later go straight on across a wide track. Some red paint marks and arrows now show the way along to the top. The path goes through a few pine trees and one copse of very large *Arbutus* trees. As another wide track is met an arrow points to the left and 7 minutes later the track ends. A short stony path then rises up to the trig point.

The red paint marks continue down the ridge to reach a col to the south-west, over granite slabs at an easy angle. Cross the col in the same direction and keep on the narrow path for a further 5 minutes. Find the wide track descending back left and indicated by another red arrow. This track crosses to the left-hand side of the valley in which are old terraces and some ruined buildings. The path descends by an old threshing floor (just off the path on the left and with a small hut at the back and a larger hut below). Continue down to reach a broad terrace with an old lemon tree. Traverse along this terrace past an abandoned house and out to the right-hand side on a wide track which goes slightly uphill. Take a left turn downhill, passing

Bridge near Alferce

a track leading to a house on the left. Seven minutes later turn left again at a T-junction, then 5 minutes later left again at another T-jjuntion. Follow the track as it swings round into the valley bottom and crosses the stream-bed.

Almost immediately, as the main track ahead starts climbing uphill, take a right turn downhill by a small house. This very soon becomes an old mule track leading in 4 minutes to a clearing. Continue in the same direction, now on a wide track again. Ten minutes later there is a 'No through road' sign pointing the way you have come from. Soon the village of Fornalha comes into sight, but before reaching it there is another left turn at a T-junction and several more bends. Then after crossing a stream-bed there is a steep pull uphill to a cultivated area on the outskirts of the village, where there is a picnic table made from a granite boulder. Ignore a right turn and pass by the post office on the left. Return to the starting point 10 minutes after going through Fornalha.

4: MONTINHOS FROM ALFERCE

Montinhos is a high point of 392m towards the end of a long ridge dividing the valley of the Odelouca from the Monchique stream. This stream is crossed twice so it is not a walk to be done after heavy rain. The valley is wild and narrow in places but the walking is mainly easy and there are views across untouched *matos*-covered hills, contrasting with areas which have been terraced and forested.

Mainly easy on good tracks. Beginning with a descent, there are two ascents of 272m and 265m. Distance: 15km. Time: about 4hrs 40mins. Map: 49D Silves and 49B S.Marcos da Serra. Grade: Moderate.

Park in the wide road on entering Alferce. Start walking into the village and follow the road as it bends left. At a T-junction with a water tap on the left turn right and keep on this road as it curves left and right again. Turn right in front of a double row of houses and go down the Rua Rossia. When the surfaced road ends follow the earth track and at the point where it doubles back towards a farm go straight on and turn left by a ruined building. Keep along this narrow path above terraced fruit trees and follow it on to a wider path on a ridge. Take a left fork, cross the ridge and meet a T-junction. Turn right, going downhill on the north side, then turn right at the next junction. In just under 10 minutes turn right onto another wider track which leads round to the south of the ridge and a minute later take a minor path left leading down to the stream.

The first time we came here there was a plank footbridge with a high handrail, but on a second visit the plank was lying useless on the far side and a refreshing paddle across the stream was needed. Go up the wide track on the other side, turning right at the first junction and right again 5 minutes later between two old buildings. The track contours into a side valley and then up to a little col with a small inhabited house on the left. There are two tracks up the ridge ahead. Take the one on the left to arrive on the ridge in just under 15 minutes. Ignore a cross track and 3 minutes later turn right at a T-juntion. Ignore a branch left and go straight on by an island in the middle of the track. This track curves round on to the west side of

Rocha de Pena. (Walk 15)

Crossing the wier below Paderne Castle (Walk 10)
Seixo (Walk 20)

the ridge and Alferce can be seen about the same height on the other side of the valley. After curving back towards the new road, join a wide track and follow it to join this road (still under construction in December 1993) and follow it up for about 10 minutes to reach the main north-south ridge.

Follow the track south along the ridge, ignoring all side tracks. After about 20 minutes the track curves right, then left again and at this point there is a major track descending into the valley used on the return. Five minutes later a rough path on the left leads uphill

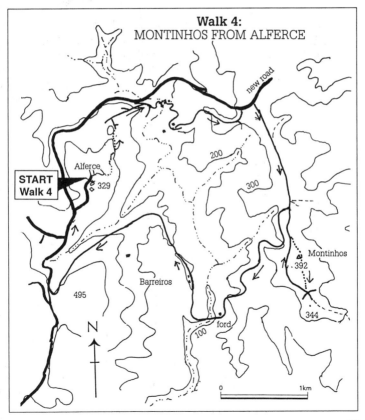

Walk 4:
MONTINHOS FROM ALFERCE

to the top of Montinhos. The trig point is surrounded by bushes and does not give the best view. Continue on past the top to the south to reach a five-way junction on a kind of col. Take the branch doubling back right uphill, then contouring to return to the descent track pointed out earlier.

Follow this down to the valley as it swings into side valleys and round spurs until the stream is met below a small house. [Note that a narrow and inviting path beginning by the house only leads to a water supply.] The main valley here is narrow with steep rocky sides and there is no path up. Instead, cross the ford a short distance downstream and follow the track leading steeply up away from the stream. It leads up to the ridge-like hill of Barreiros on which are two ruined houses. Keep to the main track, turning left at a T-junction and a few minutes later crossing a narrow neck of land. The track now climbs uphill, swinging left and looking down into a deep-cut narrow valley on the right. Eventually it vees into the head of the gully and swings right to join the road leading back to Alferce and the starting point.

5: PARRA AND THE ODELOUCA RIVER

The Parra area is a national forest (*Mata Nacional*) which is being terraced and planted with new trees, mainly eucalyptus but with some pines. It is bounded by the newly upgraded road from Silves to Son Marcos in the east and the Odelouca river in the west. The natural vegetation in this area of acid soil over underlying shales is typical *matos* with gum cistus predominant and much tree heather, gorse and arbutus. The landscape is all rolling hills either green with *matos* or reddish-ochre where the hills have been terraced and prepared for planting. The river is narrow and winding, the banks thickly vegetated with stands of alders and other trees among the giant reeds.

To reach the start of the walk from the south, cross the river bridge at Silves and turn right on the Messines road N124. After about 600m turn left on a road signposted 'Centre Saude'. Turn right at the corner of the cemetery and then right again at a T-junction. After 1km take the left fork on a road recently upgraded by EEC funds. The road to Parra is 14.7km from the cemetery and there is a wide parking area on the left-hand side of the main road bordered by eucalyptus trees.

The walking is mainly easy on wide forest roads but there is a short steep descent on a roughly bulldozed track. The river must be forded twice but even in January the water is not cold. Ascent of about 240m at the end of the walk. Distance: 10km. Time: 3hrs 30mins. Map: 49D Silves. Grade: Moderate.

Walk along the road north for about 50m, ignoring a left turn almost immediately, then turning left down the wide track towards Parra. In 20 minutes a newly restored forestry building is reached on a col. There is a track left signposted to Louro. The track on the right is the

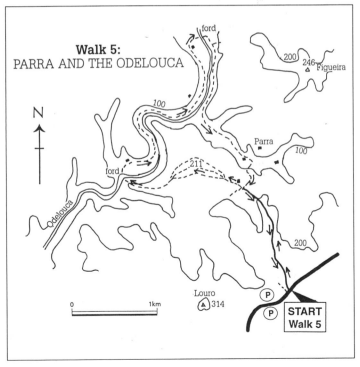

Walk 5:
PARRA AND THE ODELOUCA

one used on the return route. Ahead is a low hill (spot height 211m). Tracks go round it left and right and either could be followed, but it is more rewarding in terms of views to take the track leading straight up the brow of the hill. On the top this track ends in a ploughed area, but a bulldozed way continues down the ridge which now curves to the south-west. This is a steep but short descent soon reaching a level area where the two tracks which went round the hill meet up again. Keep going down in the same direction and another two tracks are met. Almost immediately the track ahead ends in a large turning circle, but a steep bulldozed way leads down to the river in 5 or 6 minutes.

The river is normally quite shallow at this point and easily forded. On the other side is a fragrant eucalyptus wood where the track leading to the right passes an abandoned house. Follow the track past the house to the north and then to the east as the river makes a wide meander. Turning north again the valley opens out and a cultivated area is reached. There are old terraces of fruit and vegetables and a large open field with one or two large trees left standing. The lane leads round behind a farmhouse and then returns to ford the river for a second time. Sometimes it is possible to find a crossing place that avoids getting the feet wet. A few minutes later ignore an uphill track on the left and keep straight on along the main track. This follows the river to the south then turns up left into the side valley of Parra. A boundary marker for the *Mata Nacional* is passed and 30 minutes later a low white house is reached at Parra. The road then sweeps up in several bends to reach the forest house passed on the descent.

6: ILHA DO ROSÁRIO

The river Arade and the wide Odelouca stream meet 4km west of Silves where the Arade becomes a big river. The Arade was once navigable all the way to the town of Silves, which was the capital city of the *Al-Gharb* during the Arab occupation. A walk around this town with its impressive castle is highly recommended either before or after the Ilha do Rosário walk. The area of this walk is at the junction of the two rivers where there is a small hill so bounded by watercourses that it is almost an island, hence the name Ilha de Rosário. The walk goes through orange groves and a small village

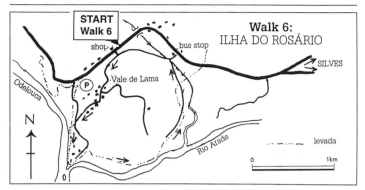

but for the most part closely follows the river banks along the side of an irrigation channel or *levada*. Trees and shrubs line the bank and in winter and early spring the paper-white narcissus will be seen flowering in profusion.

From Silves take the EN124 towards Porto de Lagos and after the road turns sharp left in 3km and goes over a bridge park opposite a shop about 300m further on.

> **Level walking along easy tracks and paths. Distance: 5.5km.**
> **Time: Allow about 2hrs or even longer to allow time for**
> **bird-watching etc. Map: 49D Silves. Grade: Very easy.**

Take the track opposite the shop and when the narrow lane is met turn right. The track goes uphill a little and through the small village of Vale da Lama then starts to descend again, heading towards the river. An ashphalted road is met and followed to the left. (This road comes in from the main road near a bend where there is parking space by some iron gates and the walk could equally well be started from here.) At the lowest point of this road cross the *levada* by a wooden bridge on the right and start walking along the narrow path on the side of it. The *levada* curves round and becomes very close to the Odelouca which at this point is wide and deep and much more a river than a stream. Herons, egrets and other birds may be seen here.

At the confluence of the rivers there is a little rocky outcrop projecting into the water with excellent views. There is an island

69

The Odelouca with Silves in the distance

ahead and the flat fields seen on the opposite bank are (or were) used for growing rice. Continue walking at the side of the *levada* which curves inland by a house with a swimming pool, the Quinta do Rosário. Ignore the surfaced road and continue along the *levada* path. After heading back towards the river, Silves comes into view at a point where the hillside was cut away during the construction of the *levada*. One or two houses with access roads are passed, but keep following the *levada* until a bridge leading to some large polythene greenhouses is reached. At this point follow the cart-track heading north. The *levada* is now on the left-hand side and then crosses overhead on concrete supports. At a junction where a narrow walled track comes in on the right, turn left and cross the bridge over the Falach stream. Follow this lane to complete the circle.

7: PARDIEIRO

Pardieiro is the highest point of an upland plateau covering a large area of the sparsely-populated hinterland between Lagos and the west coast. We are grateful to David Ormerod for supplying details of this walk which we found most enjoyable and for his permission to include it in this book. It is a walk through attractive upland scenery with extensive views over rolling hills and far removed from the tourist areas. Starting out at Barão de São Miguel (known locally simply as São Miguel), it ends at Budens (pronounced 'Boodench'), a small town with a long history dating back to the Neolithic Age. The church by the bus stop is a fine example of local sixteenth-century architecture. There are several bars and cafes and a bakery renowned for specialities based on almonds.

The route makes use of public transport from Lagos, leaving this resort either at 09.00 via Luz and Burgau, arriving at 09.35, or 10.45 via Bensafrim, arr. 11.08. There is a convenient return bus from Budens at 16.45 and another at 18.00 but this latter is only on Saturdays, Sundays and holidays from 16 September to 30 June.

Quite a long route with a gradual ascent of about 250m, all on tracks or unsurfaced roads. Distance: 17km. Time: 4hrs 45mins. Map: 52A Portimão and 51B Vila do Bispo. Grade: Moderate.

From the centre of São Miguel by the church walk south-west down the main road for 400m. Just short of the bridge turn right onto an unsurfaced road and at a five-way junction go second left. Fork first left over a stream, ignore the first track right, but go right at a cross track and curve round over a bridge. Fork left to pass a small house and a few minutes later pass a farmhouse on the left. After this there is a steady ascent to the plateau. At the top of the ascent, fork left to reach the trig point on Pardieiro at 144m. Return to this junction and now go left passing a ruined building to a junction. Go left and left again one minute later. Turn 90° left in front of a prominent white barn or cow-shed. Pass through a clump of pine trees, fork left and join a wider track coming in from the right. Keep on this track, heading generally west, and eventually descend from the end of the ridge into the valley, with the village of Pedralva ahead to the right.

71

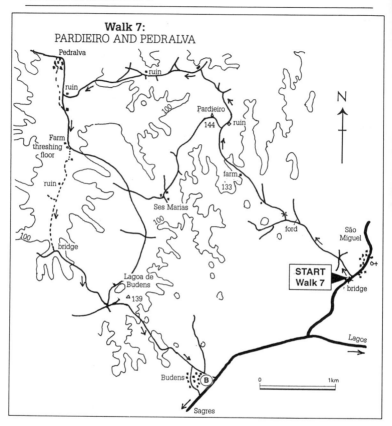

Walk 7:
PARDIEIRO AND PEDRALVA

Join a wide unsurfaced road and turn left. (Or go right to visit Pedralva where there is a bar, which may or may not have any food.)

Proceed south along the unsurfaced road, passing eucalyptuses on the right and a farm building on the left. The next farm is on the right and has a small threshing circle near the road. A hundred metres after passing this and as the road begins to climb up and bear away to the left, take the narrow path off right and descend to an old track on the left-hand side of the valley floor. At a T-junction with a newer track, go right and follow the track round to the left over a stream. Pass a ruined cottage on the right, after which there are no other landmarks for some time. Some 15 to 20 minutes after passing the ruin, turn left over a bridge, on a track leading slightly uphill into a side valley. Continue on the track, ascending to the plateau again and skirting a eucalyptus plantation, to come to a five way junction. Take the second left (slightly hidden) by a prominent pine tree (or take first left to visit Lagoa de Budens, then return). Fork right after 2 minutes and descend to a col, keeping to the left of a prominent electricity pylon, before re-ascending to a ridge beyond. The track contours round to the left then swings sharply right to pass a small cottage, before dropping down quite quickly into Budens. (In November 1993 a new road and what looked like a small housing development was being constructed here.) There are cafés in the village and the bus stop is in front of the church.

From São Miguel to Pedralva about 2hrs 30mins, Pedralva to Budens 2hrs 15mins.

Paper-white narcissus

8: ÁGUAS FRIAS AND ZAMBUJAL

These two villages lie in the Serra do Caldeirão at the north of the Algarve where it adjoins the province of Alentejo. Until 1975 they were only reached by rough tracks. Since then a surfaced road and a new bridge has rendered them more accessible but they are still remote and unspoilt. This walk provides a glimpse of Portuguese village life, where a few houses cluster round a post office and a primary school. Washing is still done in the river and almost every house is partly self-sufficient with their own chickens, pigs or goats and a vegetable plot with some fruit trees. Oak is harvested for cork and some grain is grown in clearings on the *matos*-covered hills. The route follows the upper reaches of the Arade river and from the hill-top village of Zambujal crosses a water shed to follow the Alentejo border.

To reach the start of the walk drive north from the N125 to Benafim and go straight on along the new road north. Turn left at the junction towards Monte Ruivo then at Azinhal go right and immediately left at an off-set crossroads. When Águas Frias is reached park just before the bridge.

Mainly easy walking on wide unsurfaced roads and tracks but the final descent is rough and overgrown. Some route-finding abilities called for. Distance: 11.5km. Time: About 4hrs. Maps: 49D Silves and 49B S. Marcos da Serra. Grade: Difficult.

Walk up the wide unsurfaced road to the right and immediately before the bridge in Águas Frias. This rises gently giving views down into the valley of the Arade river where areas of cultivated ground are interspersed with stands of giant reeds, poplars and oleanders. The road leaves the main valley to cross over a shoulder, where after 50 minutes' walking the village of Zambujal suddenly

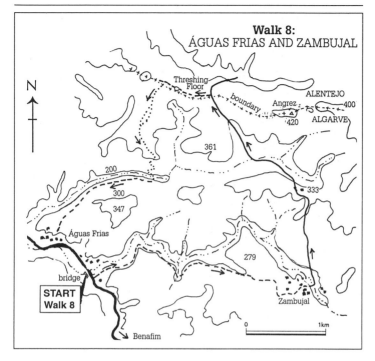

Walk 8:
ÁGUAS FRIAS AND ZAMBUJAL

comes into view. There is a short descent and then a steep rise to the centre of the village where another road is met. Turn left and follow the road downhill to cross the bridge over the Arade, turning left again after the bridge. After passing the post office the track rises up fairly steeply towards an attractive white house almost at the top of the hill. (Near spot height of 333m.) The road is lined with aromatic gum cistus and *Arbutus* bushes.

Beyond the house the road descends slightly before turning right to climb up a side valley, reaching a pass on a ridge which forms the boundary with the Alentejo. (This is indicated by a road sign saying Loulé Concelho with a line through it.) At this point the main road continues downhill and is left to take the stony track on the left which rises along a well-defined ridge. After a few minutes there is an excellent view into an attractive river valley with a few scattered houses, hillsides dotted with cork oaks among the *matos* and some cultivated fields. Continue up the ridge for about 20 minutes until a fine threshing floor is found, exactly on the line of the ridge and some 11m across. About 150m after crossing this turn sharp left along a subsidiary ridge. After about 10 minutes, where a bulldozed track goes straight up the hill ahead, take a very narrow path on the right. This is an old path marked on the map and still recognisable underfoot but extremely overgrown with gum cistus and heather. It circumnavigates the bump on the ridge and after about 10 minutes rejoins the bulldozer track.

Continue to follow this along the descending ridge, where it is rough and stony underfoot and partly overgrown. Keep on the crest of the ridge until the way ahead becomes completely barred by very dense vegetation. At this point a wide bulldozer track will be found on the right. This zigzags down rather steeply reaching the little stream in the valley bottom in about 15 minutes. Cross the stream and follow the path up to reach a wide and easy track. This makes a rising traverse up out of the valley and over a shoulder with views down into Águas Frias. Follow the track down through the houses and turn left along the road to return to the starting point by the bridge.

9: PICO ALTO

Pico Alto is a tiny village on a limestone hill of the same name some 4km east of Messines. There are outstanding views from the high road and path leading to the trig point at 276m. The vegetation here is typical of the Barrocal limestone area and includes rosemary, cistus albidus, lavender and thyme. This walk makes use of old tracks and paths and sees many aspects of rural life with intense cultivation of almonds, oranges and salad vegetables in the narrow valley between Azinhalinho and Conqueiros. The climate is mild enough to raise bananas in this area and surprisingly the almonds on the ridge were in full flower in mid-January, far earlier than the ones lower down. There are numerous examples of deep disused wells complete with rusty wheels and buckets, one to almost every house. The public washhouse in the village of Cerro is of very recent construction.

Approaching Messines from Paderne take the right turn at the

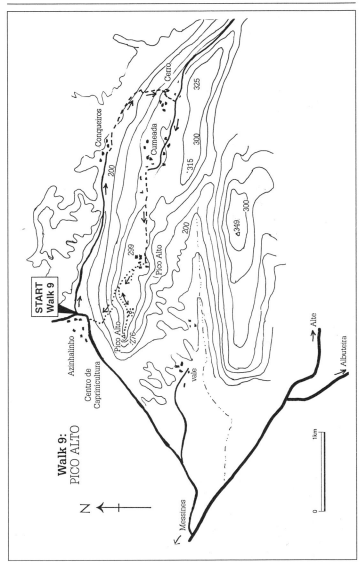

entrance to the village signposted 'Fonte J. Luis 3'. This leads to a group of houses marked as Azinhalinho on the map. After passing a track on the left signposted to 'Centro do Caprinicultura do Algarve', find a place to leave the car at the side of the road.

Most of the walking is fairly easy but some paths are narrow and stony. Distance: 9.5km. Time: About 3hrs. Map: 49D Silves. Grade: Moderate.

Start the walk by turning right along the next road which is signposted to Conqueiros. This is a pleasant unsurfaced road rising gently at the side of cultivated fields. Ignore a right turn then a left turn and go straight on through the small village which has a post office but little else. The track continues to rise gently at first and then turns sharply right uphill into the village of Cerro. After passing the large washplace on the right, turn right on the main road at the STOP sign and keep straight on through the next little village of Cumeada.

When the surfaced road comes to an end, continue walking along the track to the small village of Pico Alto where there is another post office and several houses. The track ends here, and the narrow path which goes on to the end of the ridge is found on the right, between two white houses and immediately before reaching a palm tree. When the path forks take the right-hand branch and then any other of the vague goat tracks on the right leading to the edge of the little escarpment. The path to aim for lies on the right-hand side of a low wall. After about 10 minutes a little top is reached where the views are very fine. From this point the Pico Alto trig point can be seen at the western extremity of the ridge. It is not, as might be expected, at the highest point, but about 25m lower down and at the point where the angle of slope suddenly steepens. Follow the vague path onwards across a little dip and up to the next top, keeping near the low wall. The highest point is vegetated and the path keeps to the right-hand side of the trees and shrubs, continuing downhill towards the trig point. This is reached in a further 5 minutes after passing a line of newly grafted olive trees at the side of the path.

Return along the path to the low top with the good views. Continue for about 6 or 7 minutes and before reaching a prominent stone wall, find the path leading down left at an acute angle. This continues down in the same direction for about 15 minutes, then makes a sharp turn right near a field with some prominent white fence posts. The road at Azinhal is reached after passing a deep pool on the left and a square tank with built-in washing stones on the right. Turn right to reach the starting point.

10: PADERNE CASTLE, LEITÃO AND SERRA GRANDE

Paderne is a picturesque village 13km north-east of Albufeira and lies in a richly cultivated valley surrounded by low hills. The old castle lies 2km to the south, strategically placed on a hill-top at a bend in the river. The origins of this castle are Moorish, but it was re-built in the Middle Ages. Recently there has been some discussion about restoring it as a tourist attraction. There is a separate tower near the entrance connected to the main building by an arched gateway. Within the walls are a ruined chapel but little else remains. Below the castle there is a Roman bridge with three arches, near the ruins of an old mill. Leitão is a small hill of 154m just south of Paderne and with excellent views, well worth the short diversion it entails.

Paderne

The second half of this walk follows quiet country lanes to a tiny village called Casas de Poco. The return route follows the ridge of the 227m hill of Serra Grande south-east of Paderne with attractive views of the surrounding country. Some interesting abandoned houses, partly in ruins, are passed on the way down. A shorter return route can be made by going through the village of Cerro Grande.

This is an easy walk all on country lanes and wide tracks except for a steep and rough path near the castle, which could be avoided. Distance: 14.5km. Time: 4hrs 15mins. Map: 49D Silves. Grade: Easy.

Approach Paderne from Boliqueime on the N270 and park on the right hand side of the road just before the sign for Cerca Velha. (This is where the local bus parks so keep well in to one side.) Start walking back towards Boliqueime and take the signposted track to Barradinho. After about 10 minutes go straight on where the main track bends left. Ignore two tracks on the right. After turning 90° right and passing a row of houses the track makes a 90° left turn at the side of a wall. Going slightly downhill and crossing a shallow valley the track then meets a T-junction. Turn left and 2 minutes later turn sharp left, passing a new villa with a walled garden, Casa Norinha. The track bends right and goes alongside the garden wall. When a major track is met turn left and then bend right, going under the new motorway. The main track then swings up left to go to the castle and this way can be followed if preferred. A more direct way, albeit a little more strenuous, is to go straight on across the dry stream-bed and 2 minutes later take the narrow path on the left leading steeply up to the castle in about 5 minutes.

After looking at the castle return to the point of entry and follow the narrow path below the castle wall on the south-east side. This gradually descends to the river and part way down either the left fork or the right fork can be taken. Both lead to the river bank and the left one is the more direct but a little steeper. When the river bank is reached turn left, following a somewhat overgrown path among oleanders and giant reeds to reach the Roman bridge in about 10 minutes. Cross the bridge and turn right along a good path leading

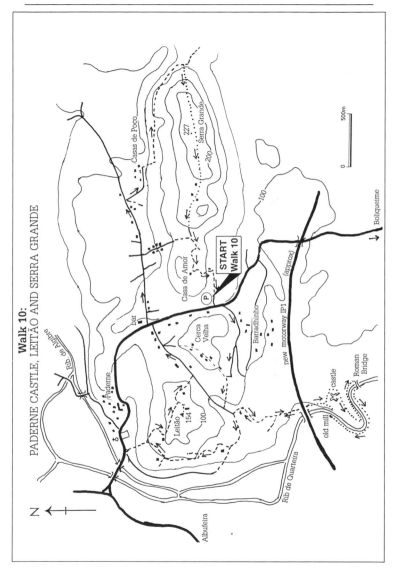

Walk 10:
PADERNE CASTLE, LEITÃO AND SERRA GRANDE

in about 15 minutes to an old mill by a weir. The house here has been restored and there is a shelter and a fireplace which can be used for picnics.

Cross the river by the old water-worn stones. These were bone dry in February but under an inch of water in November after some heavy rain and a little slippery. Follow the track back under the motorway bridge and along the outward route as far as the T-junction by the new villa. Turn left here and about 5 minutes later fork right uphill by an old abandoned house. Ten minutes later keep to the right of some blocks of apartments, to reach the crest of the hill with a view of the Rocha de Pena further to the north. Continue downhill towards Paderne, seen across almond orchards making a dazzling display of pink and white blossom in late January and February. Do not go right into Paderne but take the first right turn leading uphill to Quinta Leitão. After passing the gates of the Quinta the track bends left and right to reach a T-junction. At this point make the diversion to the top of Leitão by turning right, then right again to reach the trig point mounted on a sort of tower, the door to which is locked. Return to where the diversion began and continue along the track to another T-junction, turning left again. Keep straight on past some houses to reach the main road by a cluster of letter boxes.

At this point the walk can be shortened by turning right to reach the starting point in about 600m. (Turning left there is a small bar at the roadside serving excellent coffee.) To continue the walk turn left towards Paderne and then immediately right, signed to Almeijoefras and Monho Novo. Ignore two tracks to the right, go straight on at a crossroads and ignore another right turn opposite a house with bougainvillea cascading over the walls. Turn right at the next junction signposted 'Casas de Poco' and follow the road to this little village.

From Casas de Poco the road becomes a track and turns right and then left. Keep on the main track downhill between fields of almonds, olives and carobs for about 10 minutes, then take a track on the right by a sign 'Serra Grande' painted on a rock. This track swings round to the right to the foot of the east ridge of the hill. Look out for the track on the right leading steeply up to the ridge. The original old track between two stone walls exactly on the line of the ridge is overgrown at first so follow the tractor track at the edge of the ploughed field. In about 10 minutes the original track is joined and followed along the crest of the ridge and soon reaches a group of old abandoned houses. A little further on there is a new house and then the track goes downhill. At a T-junction turn left following the sign saying Casa de Amor 300m. In front of the Casa de Amor take a left branch track going downhill to a field barn where the track turns right. This leads back to the starting point in 5 minutes.

11: ESPARGAL AND THE RIVER ALGIBRE

Espargal is a prominent 351m hill in the limestone area north of Faro. The views from the top are panoramic and include a fine vista of the Rocha de Pena with its long line of cliffs. There is a tiny village just below the summit in which the gardens are a colourful mass of spring and summer flowers such as violets, stocks, canna lilies, roses and geraniums, all flowering in February. The village is accessible by a minor road from the east, but this walk approaches from the south after first following the course of the Ribiera de Algibre from the village with the same name.

The first part of the valley is flat-floored and richly cultivated with olives, carobs, vines, almonds and peaches. Peas and beans are well-advanced in January. Almost every field has its own well. Giant reeds, *Arundo donax*, grow by the river. Normally the water level is very low and in places completely dry, but there are signs particularly in the narrow section that it is sometimes in spate when this walk would not be possible.

The area between Espargal and the river is a sloping hillside which is partly cultivated, growing carobs and almonds, and partly wild, with lime-loving plants like rosemary and cistus. There are numerous tracks winding through this part, but unfortunately the one shown on the map as linking the line of old limekilns from Espargal to the north side of the Algibre road bridge no longer exists. It would have made a good circular walk.

To reach the starting point take the road north from Fonte de Boliqueime on the N125 and take the left turn signposted to Parragil just after passing a large quarry. Turn left at a T-junction then go straight on at a crossroads. Park at the end of the village of Ribeira de Algibre about 100m before the bridge. (Avoid this walk on

Sundays; it is very popular with hunters.)

Mainly on good tracks, but there are no waymarks. 250m of ascent. Distance: 19.5km. Time: About 5hrs. Map: 50C S. Brás de Alportel. Grade: Moderate.

Take the track which runs west along the south side of the river. Almost immediately fork right and keep on this track between cultivated fields. After 15 minutes join another track and turn right in front of a small fieldhouse, between stone walls. Further on there is a stone wall on the left which measures a good 3m across; a monument to those who cleared the land of stones. After about 35 minutes a ruined house is reached. One minute later pass a track on the right leading to a river crossing and 3 minutes later ignore a wide track on the left. After crossing a stream-bed the path heads back towards the river and then follows it closely. An old mill building is passed, almost in the river and half filled with silt. Beyond the mill there are other ruined buildings and signs of previous cultivation such as old vines growing against a wall and neglected orange trees on a grassy terrace. There is a deep empty well. For a while the track narrows and is a little overgrown, with giant celandines and paper-white narcissi growing in the shade of quite dense trees and shrubs: holm oak, wild olives, lentisc, carobs, gorse and cistus to mention but a few.

In about 20 minutes a large ruined house is seen with several old orange trees in the flat field next to the river. Go past the house to join a wide and stony track and turn right along it to cross the river. (No bridge.) Ignore a branch left. The main track curves left behind a ruined building. Turn left by an island of rocks and shrubs in the middle of the track and then take a left fork. Ignore a branch right after 30 minutes. (This is the return route.) Keep on the main track as it rises then crosses a flat area with newly planted orange trees. It curves right and contours on the north side of Espargal. Ignore the first road slanting back right, which ends at a group of houses. After passing the post office take the road on the right leading back uphill at an acute angle and fork left opposite a water tap. Continue up the old path by some steps and continue until a narrow earth path is met. Turn right here and then left up past a ruined building.

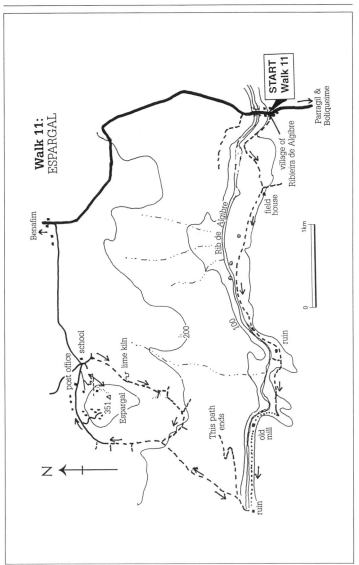

Walk 11: ESPARGAL

START Walk 11

Parragil & Boliqueime

village of Ribieira de Algibre

Rib de Algibre

field house

Benafim

school

post office

lime kiln

351△ Espargal

This path ends

old mill

ruin

ruin

N ←

1km

0

200

100

85

Continue upwards towards the top, skirting the left edge of a small almond orchard and crossing another to reach a rocky path leading to the summit.

Return down the path to the road near the post office and then turn right at the cross roads by the school. After 50m take the left fork and in a further 50m turn right. Keep right again and after 10 minutes pass a limekiln on the left. After a further 10 minutes notice a minor track off right and then 2 minutes later the main track makes a sharp bend right, with a less-used track coming in on the left. A flat area with almond trees is reached. At a T-junction turn right and follow the track as it turns west and north-west and slightly uphill to join the route of ascent. Turn left and return the same way to the starting point.

12: FUNCHAIS HILL

This flat-topped hill of about 300m lies in the limestone area south of Salir. It has no significant top but forms a broad east-west ridge with low-growing vegetation permitting views of the surrounding area. The area is rich in wild flowers with an abundance of rosemary and the two cistus plants, *albidus* and *monspeliensis* which are always indicative of limestone country. Others in flower in early February include honeysuckle, French lavender, lithospermum (or lithodorus) and miniature daffodils. Two limekilns in very good condition are passed. The return is through cultivated farmland and three small villages called Vicentes, Caliços and Funchais.

To reach the start of the walk drive north from Fonte de Boliqueime through Parragil to Ribeira de Algibre and take the first turn right after the bridge signposted to Tor and Querença. Look out for a large house on the left with a balustraded wall about 2km along this road. The walk begins 300m beyond this house at a point where the road bends to the right.

An easy walk along well-defined tracks and on a country road, which is exceptionally quiet on Saturdays when there is no quarry traffic. About 160m of fairly gentle ascent. Distance: 11km. Time: 3hrs. Map: 50C S. Brás de Alportel. Grade: Easy.

Well on descent to Funchais

Walk up the stony track towards the first limekiln which can be clearly seen ahead. After about 10 minutes a short diversion can easily be made to look at this. The track continues to climb uphill and then makes a sharp right turn, dipping and rising and then traversing below some small rocky outcrops. After bending to the left the track begins to rise again, then makes a sharp bend left at a T-junction. The direction is now west towards the trig point on Espargal (361m) which can be seen straight ahead. A few minutes later Pica Vessa (316m) is seen. After swinging north and then north-west a T-junction is met, with a pile of stones on the left. Turn right and in 10m reach a small clearing with the track continuing straight on. The top of the hill is about 100m north from here and consists of a small flat field hidden from view by some trees and shrubs. It can be reached by winding between the shrubs slightly to the east of the top.

Return to the clearing and take the track towards the east. It goes between walled fields of almond trees and then makes an acute left turn to follow the wall on the left, dropping down now towards the north. At the next T-junction turn right and follow the track into an

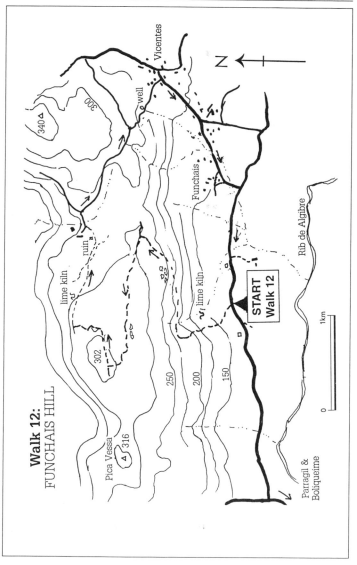

Walk 12:
FUNCHAIS HILL

French lavender

area of stone walls with some open clearings and a few almond trees. After a bend right and then another back left there are some large almond groves and an open grassy area. Another limekiln may be noticed quite near the track on the left. Later an old overgrown track between stone walls will be seen on the right; on the left are fields of peas and beans.

One minute after passing a ruin on the left a T-junction is met, the road on the left leading to a farm. Turn right and then right again at the next T-junction. There is some scrub on the rising ground left and flat fields with more almond trees below on the right. Over the ridge the track dips into a little hollow and rises again. Take the next turn right where the main track swings left. There is a painted arrow on a boulder at the beginning of this track which swings down towards a group of houses, passing a deep well on the left.

Beyond the houses turn right at a T-junction and follow the surfaced road into Vicentes. Five minutes later take the right fork signposted to Funchais and Ribeira de Algibre. Go through Caliços to reach Funchais, where there is a bar, the Café Mario, on the right hand side of the road. Five minutes later turn right along the main road to return to the starting point in 20 minutes.

13: BARRANQUINHO AND PORTELA

Barranquinho is a deserted village and Portela is a small hamlet, both lying on a limestone hill south of the Benafim-Salir road. The highest point of the hill, the Cabeça de Areia at 377m, is crowned by a ruined windmill, the thick walls of which stand above the surrounding trees and provide a superb viewpoint. To the north is the Rocha de Pena and to the south-west is Espargal. The ridge is covered with typical lime-loving plants with rosemary predominating. The approach from Salir crosses the fertile valley

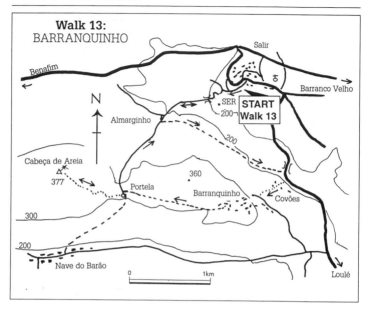

Walk 13:
BARRANQUINHO

below the town with its orange and almond groves and a fascinating variety of old wells and irrigation channels. At Barranquinho only two of the old houses appear to be occupied and another two restored as holiday homes; the rest are totally deserted.

Salir lies 16km north of Loulé. Entering from the Benafim direction take the right fork and after 500m go straight on (signposted Loulé) when the main road swings left. Park on this wide road near the 'Perigo Escola' sign.

> **Mostly easy walking on good tracks and paths, but the old path between Covões and Barranquinho has been partly destroyed by ploughing and is rough and difficult to follow. 200m of ascent. Distance: 10km. Time: About 3hrs 30mins. Map: 50C S. Brás de Alportel. Grade: Moderate.**

Turn back and go down the lane next to the school sign with a signpost SER. (SER is an international drug rehabilitation centre for young people situated in the valley below.) The track goes down to the stream which is crossed by a bridge, continuing across the flat valley floor to arrive at a T-junction in a group of houses. Turn right, then immediately left, by a large sign saying Fonte Figueira. Then take the first left again. This road soon becomes an unsurfaced track and is pleasant walking (except after rain when the red earth becomes very sticky). There are good views across the valley to Salir.

When the main road is reached between two buildings at Covões, turn right and after 100m turn right again up a steep track. This appears to end at a house, but turn left and in a few yards look out for a narrow path on the right. This rises up steadily to join the narrow lane leading to Barranquinho from the Nave do Barão road. In the winter of 1993 this had been recently ploughed in places but could still be followed; whether it will be re-established or completely lost is difficult to say. An alternative if necessary or if preferred is to continue along the main road and then turn right towards Nave de Barão, and take the first right again.

Turn right along the narrow road to go through Barranquinho. After several bends this road starts to go downhill. At this point turn right up an old track at the side of a wall. This traverses the hillside to reach Portela, passing on the way a group of ruined houses. Among them is a thriving smallholding with many fruit and almond trees. After a few bends this track joins a surfaced road.

Turn left to reach the top of the pass at Portela in a few minutes. From the turning circle at the end of the surfaced road turn right up a wide track, passing some beehives. After a group of carob trees this track dwindles to a narrow path which leads to the top. On the almost flat ground near the top it becomes a little vague, but the top of the old windmill can be spotted ahead and gives the direction. Iron rungs on the outer wall can easily be climbed to enjoy the view from the top.

Return to Portela by the same path and turn left down the road to Fonte Figueira. Turn right and then left to return to Salir across the footbridge used on the way out.

14: PENA WINDMILLS FROM BRAZIEIRA

These two white windmills are in a prominent position on the easterly continuation of the Rocha de Pena ridge and can easily be approached from Pena (see Walk 15). The short walk described here could be combined with a visit to Salir, an attractive village which was once a Moorish stronghold and having a ruined castle and a church which boasts an illuminated manuscript dated 1530. This approach to the windmills from the north goes up a semi-wild valley where there are some cork oaks among the *matos* and descends through a cultivated valley in which lie the three small hamlets of Brazieira: Cima, Maia and Baixo (Upper, Middle and Lower). There are excellent views from the windmills. One of these is in ruins. The other still has some of the working parts on top but is locked up.

To reach the start of the walk drive towards Salir from Benafim and take a minor road left before getting into the town. After about 1.5km park near the first house on the left-hand side of the road by a bridge over the Brazieira stream.

A short walk on easy tracks and with an ascent of about 130m. Distance: 3.5km. Time: 1hr. Map: 50C S Bras de Alportel. Grade: Easy.

Cross the bridge and immediately take a left turn, ignoring the narrow path which also begins here. Follow the wide track uphill through an area of cork oaks. There are signs of old cultivation terraces among the *matos*. After a steady ascent of about 15 minutes the track swings right and meets a T-junction with a ruined building on the right. Turn left uphill on a little ridge between the two valleys. That on the left is in a semi-natural state and that on the right is highly cultivated. Two minutes later take a left fork, then turn right at a T-junction to reach the main track leading to the windmills from the Pena valley. Turn right to reach the windmills in a further 5 minutes.

Continue on the wide track past the windmills and in about 50m turn right down the wide earthen track. After 10 minutes' steady descent the track reaches the small hamlet of Brazieira de Meio and turns right then left between the houses. Five minutes later take a right turn by a house with a garage door currently painted bright

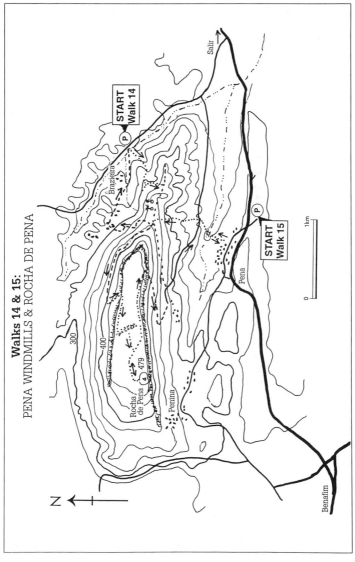

Walks 14 & 15:
PENA WINDMILLS & ROCHA DE PENA

START Walk 14

START Walk 15

Salir

Brazieira

Rocha de Pena ▲ 479

Penina

Pena

Benafim

300

400

N

0   1km

blue. The lane now descends through cork oaks and cereal crops with small patches of peas, beans and cabbages all flourishing in the winter months. About 10 minutes later take a right fork. There is a building on the right and another track leading to some more houses. The main track continues descending along the right-hand side of a narrow valley with a stream on the left to reach the bridge where the walk began.

15: ROCHA DE PENA

The Rocha is a prominent limestone hill north of the small village of Pena which is 4km west of Salir. It has a long flat top with steep cliffs on the north and south, those on the south providing the only rock-climbing in the Algarve. The views from the top at 479m and from the edges of the plateau are extensive. The top is covered with *matos* (mainly gum cistus) but with much rosemary and other plants which thrive on limestone. In January also there are tiny miniature daffodils about 4 inches high and many clumps of paper-white narcissi. Two pairs of Bonelli's eagles nest in the area and may often be seen soaring up the cliffs.

Although this walk is partly on easy tracks there is a short steep scramble up to the plateau on the north side. About 230m of ascent. Distance: 10km. Time: 3hrs 45mins. Map: 50C S. Brás de Alportel. Grade: Moderate.

Park on the wide verge of the main road above the village of Pena and at the east end. Walk down the narrow road into the village and look out for the communal washplace which is down a short branch on the right. Just before reaching the washplace turn right to find the track leading down to the bridge over the Moinho stream. Turn right at the surfaced road and then immediately left up a narrow track lined with small shrubs of narrow-leaved cistus. There is a farm on the right and storage ponds of reddish water on both sides of the track. After 10 to 12 minutes of fairly steep uphill there is a major cross-track, with a rough Land-rover track straight ahead. At this point it is worth a short diversion right to look at the two prominent white windmills on the ridge. (See Walk 14.)

To continue, return to this point and go up the steep track now

Paper-white Narcissi

on the right. This levels out and traverses along the north side of the escarpment arriving after about 15 minutes at a noticeboard with the words 'Zona de Caza Turistica'. Immediately by this sign is a narrow path sloping back up from right to left and making for the lowest part of the escarpment rocks which are reached in a little over 10 minutes. Once on the top turn right and follow the northern edge of the escarpment along narrow winding paths between the dense shrubs. When these become too dense near the edge, other paths further inland can be found. After about 30 minutes a rampart of large stones extending right across the plateau will be reached. This is believed to date from the Bronze Age. From this point a large square clearing can be seen ahead with a track leading up towards the right-hand side of the trig point. Either make straight through the *matos* towards this, or for easier walking turn and walk along the top of the boulders for a few minutes until you see one of several paths leading to the clearing.

From the clearing it is only 10 minutes further to the top. Follow the wide track up until some low stone walls are reached. Turn left

Orange tree near Pena

between the first two of these and follow a narrow and very winding path through dense scrub and trees to reach the top.

Return the same way to the clearing and cross it towards the left-hand side of a carob tree at the southern edge. Follow the edge of the escarpment along a pleasant path with good views of the crags. There is a slight rise towards the large rampart of stones. Shortly beyond the stones and on the left it is worth making a short diversion to a cave. Continuing onwards a large cleared area with low stone walls is passed, possibly signs of earlier habitation. When a red earth track with a carob tree in the centre is reached, turn right and follow this down below the cliffs. (At the point where it turns left a cairn and arrow mark a climber's path up to the cliffs.) When the surfaced road is reached turn left. At this point there is a *fonte* built round a carob tree and a signpost to 'Rocha de Pena' useful to anyone wishing to reverse this walk. Follow the surfaced road for about 15 minutes then turn right and follow the path back to Pena used at the start of the walk.

Near the Guadiana river (Walk 23)
Cliff path, Pontal (Walk 27)

River and beach of Bordeira, north of Pontal (Walk 27)
On cliffs north of Cape St Vincent (Walk 30)

16: FONTE DE BENÉMOLA AND TWO CAVES

This spring is in the sheltered valley of the Ribeira dos Moinhos, south of Salir and west of the attractive little village of Querença. The walk is best done after some rain, when water can be seen welling up from the depths of the pool. This pool has been made by damming the river and in 1993 new shrubs had been planted all around, but there was no sign of the picnic tables described in the information leaflet. The valley is one of the Algarve's protected areas of natural beauty and is full of birdsong and a good place for wild flowers. It is not wild, but cultivated with orange trees, carobs, nysperas and small vegetable plots. Although well publicised and signposted it is surprisingly quiet and peaceful. The two caves or *grutas* are situated in a small escarpment above the spring, overlooking the valley to the south. The second one reached is the larger and there is an inner cave reached by going either left or right of a central pillar.

The start is reached by driving north from the N125 at Fonte de Boliqueime, turning left to Parragil, left at a T-junction, straight on at a crossroads, then turning right after the bridge over the Ribeira de Algibre. Go straight on at Tor towards Querença. About 2km after Tor the road crosses a river bridge and turns sharp left under an unsightly quarry face. The road then swings right and 150m later the signposted track will be seen on the left, where there is some parking.

> A gentle easy walk with an ascent of less than 80m. The path descending from the caves to the spring is rough and rocky. After heavy rains the ford may be impassable and then the return would have to be by the outward route. Distance: 6km. Time: About 2hrs. Map: 50C S. Brás de Alportel. Grade: Moderate (or Easy if caves are excluded).

Start walking along the track passing an abandoned house in front of which is a large threshing circle about 16m in diameter. The Fonte Menalva stream can be heard running in the valley below, where there are tiny cultivated fields between the evergreen foliage of the olives, carobs and nysperas and the high stands of the giant reeds, *Arundo donax*. Ignore a branch track right leading to a house as the

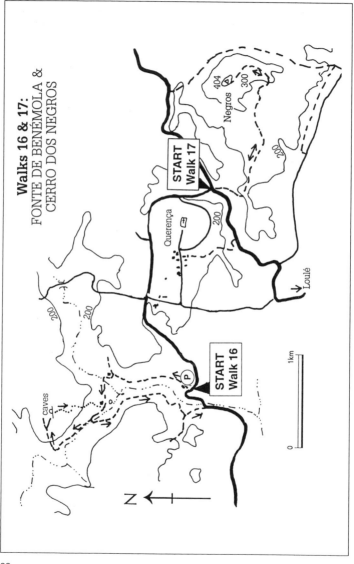

Walks 16 & 17:
FONTE DE BENÉMOLA &
CERRO DOS NEGROS

track curves left to cross a sidestream, the Ribeira da Chapa. Ignore another branch right, going straight on along the river bank to reach the spring.

To continue to the caves, walk along the wide track at the side of the stream, passing the ford used on the return route after about 150m. The river valley narrows and there is an outcrop of steep but vegetated limestone high up on the left. When the valley widens again the track bends right and starts climbing uphill. Take the first branch right. After 100m it becomes a narrow path leading immediately to the two caves.

To return to the spring, follow the narrow but well-defined path slanting down directly from the second cave. The descent takes about 10 to 12 minutes. Turn right and cross the ford which is usually dry. There are pleasant views down into the valley again, with giant celandines and large clumps of the blue periwinkle, *Vinca difformis*, growing in the shade. Two small houses are passed with many dogs, friendly but extremely noisy. One or two wells or *noras* with metal scoop wheels will be noticed. Ignore a left turn where the track rises slightly and goes through an area of cork oaks before reaching the road near the bridge. Turn left to return to the starting point, passing a disused mill with an interesting system of leats.

17: CERRO DOS NEGROS

The Cerro dos Negros at 404m is a superb viewpoint. North of Loulé, this walk can easily be combined with a visit to the weekly market, or can be done after the previous walk to the Fonte de Benémola and include a visit to the hilltop village of Querença. Just outside the region of the Barrocal limestone it has views over much of the area including the Rocha de Pena which is the most conspicuous and striking of all the tops. To the north and east the landscape is quite different from the limestone area with *matos*-covered shale hills growing cork oaks. In winter and early spring splashes of colour are provided by the abundant white and pink heathers. On the summit there is a double form of the ubiquitous Bermuda buttercup.

The start of the walk is immediately opposite the Querença road junction on the EN396, about 12km north of Loulé.

Easy walking up a wide and almost drivable track, but a steep pull up of almost 300m. Distance: 5km. Time: 1hr 45mins. Map: 50C S. Bras de Alportel. Grade: Moderate.

The track is signposted 'Cerro dos Negros, 404m' with a picture of binoculars to indicate a viewpoint. Simply follow the main track ignoring branches right and left. Return the same way. (Note that the track up this hill is not shown at all on the published maps so the sketch map is only an approximation.)

18: CIRCUIT OF CABEÇA GORDA

Cabeça Gorda is a low limestone hill with open views, near the town of Loulé which has a good weekly market, worth visiting before the walk. The area is typical of the Barrocal limestone with smallholdings growing almonds, carobs and figs, while the hill itself has the characteristic lime-loving plants of rosemary, cistus and so on. A very good example of a limekiln is seen near the abandoned house of Cabeça Gorda, where an old carob tree growing out of a rocky mound is an attractive feature.

The walk begins from the EN396 at a small village called Barreiras Brancas. Approaching from Loulé it is easy to park under some trees at the side of the road immediately after passing the post office.

A very easy walk on wide tracks which are a little stony in places. Distance: 5.5km. Time: 1hr 45mins. Map: 50C S. Bras de Alportel. Grade: Very Easy.

Take the old track to the south-east which begins opposite a snack bar adjacent to the post office. At first it is between houses but very soon comes to open fields. Go over a small bridge and ignore all branches to the right. Further on there is a large stone wall on the left and an abandoned house with a typical latticed chimney on the right. Take a left fork half a minute after passing this house. The track now rises uphill and as it levels out again the limekiln will be seen on the left shortly before reaching the house Cabeça Gorda.

The track continues beyond the house and gradually curves round to the north side of the hill with extensive views right across to Rocha de Pena. When the track begins to descend slightly look

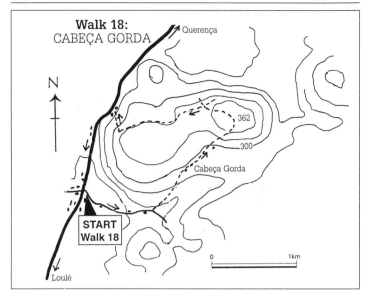

Walk 18:
CABEÇA GORDA

Querença

N

362

300

Cabeça Gorda

START
Walk 18

Loulé

0   1km

out for a circular clearing with a cross-track. Turn left along a good path which is really an overgrown track, with a low stone wall at the right-hand side. As it swings round to the south Loulé comes into view and there are a few large limestone outcrops. The track then curves to the right, passing a group of umbrella pines before descending to join the road by some new houses. Turn left for a 1km walk along the road to return to the starting point.

19: PARIZES - FEITERA - PARIZES

The undulating hills of the Serra de Alcaria do Carne are a delightful walking area, being sparsely populated and having a varied landscape of many ridges and hills intersected by small streams and some quite large rivers. It is of special interest as an area where cork is harvested. Near the small mountain villages the land is cultivated but elsewhere there is dense *matos* among which are patches of the very attractive tree heathers in pink and white, with yellow gorse and strawberry trees bearing both flowers and fruit. Roads and tracks often follow ridges with narrower paths descending into the valleys, so that walks in this area often involve river crossings as this one does. This circular walk crosses the river Odeleite twice, so it is not recommended after heavy rain when the crossings may be impassable.

Parizes is about 25km north of Faro and is reached by taking the newly surfaced hill road from the main S. Brás to Lisbon road (EN2). Turn right at Alportel and go through Cova da Muda and Javalis. Park anywhere on the road near the village of Parizes.

Most of the walking is on easy tracks and paths, but skill in trail-finding is needed for part of the return route on a narrow and overgrown path. The route begins with a descent and there are two ascents totalling 390m. Distance: 9.4km. Time: about 3hrs 45mins. Map: 50C S. Brás de Alportel. Grade: Moderately Difficult.

Take the road through the village (west) immediately opposite the water pump and after one minute fork left. Then fork right by a memorial cross where the road becomes unsurfaced. The track descends to the river through cork oaks, areas of cultivated land and patches of gum cistus. Cross the river by the rather pointed stepping stones and follow the track which climbs steadily uphill in a

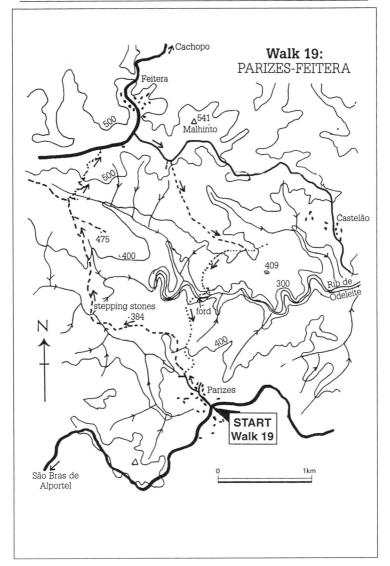

Cachopo

Walk 19:
PARIZES-FEITERA

Feitera

500

△541
Malhinto

Castelão

500

475

‹400

409

300

Rib de
Odeleite

stepping stones
·384

ford

N

400

Parizes

**START
Walk 19**

São Bras de
Alportel

△

0   1km

northerly direction. Ignore a track which slopes back to the right and about 45 minutes after crossing the river look for a narrow path descending to the right. This is found immediately opposite a wide track on the left by a marker stone with initials JBL. Almost immediately take a left fork and continue dropping down between head-high *matos* to reach a small clear stream in the valley-bottom in about 5 minutes. There is a small walled area with a single orange tree and signs of some previous cultivation.

Cross the stream and go up the steep rocky path straight ahead. The path then zigzags up more gently and there are traces of a wall at the edge. Ignore a cross-track. When the path levels off and the road on the ridge can be seen ahead, the path becomes a little indistinct. Continue walking parallel to the road and pick up a wider track among the cork oaks. This joins the main road opposite another track where a ruined windmill may be noticed up among the trees on the other side of the road. Turn right and continue along the road for 400m to reach the outskirts of Feitera.

Turn right along the road signposted to Castelão. On either side of the road are stacked large piles of cork awaiting collection. One pile almost completely covered the village football pitch in the winter of 1993. Walk along this road for about 5 minutes until it makes a very pronounced bend to the left. Be careful not to take the branch track just before the bend but continue until the wide and well-made track descending towards the valley is reached. Keep on this main track ignoring side branches until after about 10 minutes it swings to the left. Two minutes later take a right fork uphill at first and in another 10 minutes look out for a very narrow path on the right-hand side which doubles back sharply. This path leaves the track at a point 100m before a large and solitary oak tree. Although this path is narrow, overgrown and little used it is the only turning at this point. Follow it along and then down through high *matos* to reach an extremely large cork oak. After this the path becomes more indistinct but will be found to lead from one oak to another until it reaches a stony stream-bed by another large oak. After this the path rises again and almost disappears, but the trace of it can be followed as it bends left and descends steadily to the river. Turn right along a stone wall before finally reaching the river bank. As the river is approached note the position of the path rising up the other side as it is less easy to locate it from below. Turn right along the river bank to find a crossing place slightly upstream where there are some natural stepping stones.

The upward path begins between a sidestream and a stone wall. After about 15 minutes two enormous piles of stones are passed on the left and then a cross track is met on a ridge. Turn left and a few minutes later re-join the main track which was followed at the beginning of the walk. Turn left to return to Parizes.

20: ALCARIA ALTA AND SEIXO FROM CURRAIS

The hilltop hamlet of Alcaria Alta is near the 506m trig point of Tremoços and Seixo (pronounced 'Saysh') is a tiny settlement in the valley of the Leitejo stream. This circular walk begins in the village of Currais (pronounced 'Koo-raysh') which is 2km south of Cachopo. There are panoramic views of rolling hills, mainly in their natural state, covered with a dark green blanket of gum cistus patterned with the brighter green of *Arbutus unedo*, the strawberry tree. Elsewhere the hillsides have been cleared and terraced, exposing the reddish earth, on which there are newly planted pine trees. There are two stream crossings, one by a low bridge and the other by natural stepping stones, so this is a walk to be avoided after heavy rain.

To reach the start, take the right turn into Currais about 1km before reaching Cachopo on the N124 from Barranco Velho. On reaching the village of Currais turn right at a T-junction and park by the side of the road near the village washplace.

Mainly easy walking on wide tracks, but the descent to Seixo is by an old and little-used path which is partly overgrown and a little rough. There are two descents, with a total ascent of about 475m. Distance: 14.5km. Time: About 5hrs. Map: 50C S. Brás de Alportel. Grade: Moderate.

Start walking away from the village along the lane past the washplace. Ignore minor branches on the left and in under 10 minutes an angled crossroads is reached. Go straight on, slightly downhill and follow this track down to the stream crossing, ignoring a right branch as the main track swings left at a saddle. The stream is crossed by a raised

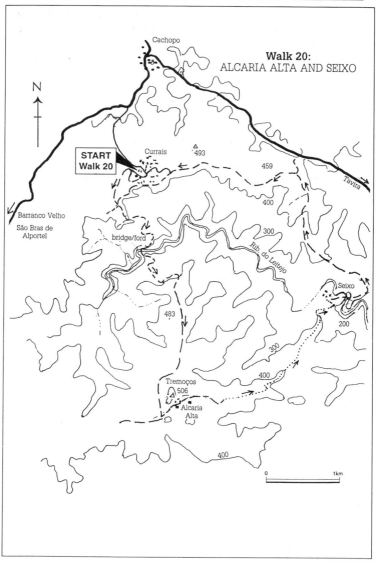

Cachopo

Walk 20:
ALCARIA ALTA AND SEIXO

N

Currais

493

459

Tavira

**START
Walk 20**

400

Barranco Velho
São Bras de
Alportel

bridge/ford

300

Rib do Leitejo

Seixo

200

483

300

300

400

Tremoços
506

400

Alcaria
Alta

400

0   1km

ford, the central part of which forms a bridge. The valley here is a little oasis with luxuriant vegetation and many birds.

The wide track now climbs steadily upwards and after a hairpin bend reaches a ridge which is followed to the south, skirting the side of a 483m hill. The trig point on Tremoços comes into view and to reach it the track swings west and then round to the south side of it. The top is reached 2 minutes after joining another track coming in from the west. Continue the walk by the track going east and downhill on the left side of a large white house. Ignore a left turn to a hill top and continue to a col and then straight on to the ridge. The track goes over a little top and then about 15 minutes later the descending ridge splits into two branches. Turn left here to get on to the left branch, avoiding the better track leading right. There is not much of a path for a while, where it has been invaded by gum cistus, but after going over another top and descending another path joins and the going improves.

The path leads down to Seixo, reaching first some ruins and two threshing floors on a spur at the end of the ridge. From here it curves back left to the inhabited houses below, passing an enormous cork oak. A young man and his mother came out to greet us; visitors must be quite rare in this remote place. From the houses the track goes down to the Leitejo stream which is shallow and easily crossed by low natural stepping stones. Near a small cultivated field take the main track which goes left and uphill. Continue up this hill to reach a col after about one hour. Do not take the left turn on this col but continue along the same way for a further 6 minutes, getting quite near the main road which can be seen ahead. Turn left and follow the main track back to Currais. It has a tendency to keep to the crests of several small hills before arriving back at Currais. Go through a gap in the wall on the right and follow the lane back down through the village to return to the starting point.

21: GARCIA, MONCHIQUE AND AMOREIRA

These three small unspoilt villages lie in the hills north-east of Cachopo. Cachopo is in the north-eastern area of the Algarve, roughly 35km north-north-east of Faro, reached from the N124 via either Loulé or São Brás de Alportel. (The village of Monchique is not to be confused with the town of the same name in the western Algarve.) They are linked by roads and tracks at a height of about 300m, providing extensive views over the surrounding countryside. The valley of the Odeleite lies below to the south-east and the valley of the Foupanilha to the north-west. All around is open country with mixed vegetation. There are almond and olive groves, cereal crops and rough grazing for sheep and goats as well as areas of untouched *matos*. Some of the hillsides have been cleared and terraced ready for planting eucalyptus. Elsewhere there are old stands of cork oaks and umbrella pines. Traditional agricultural methods are still used; ploughing is with a horse or mule and threshing floors are still in use.

To reach the start, drive to Cachopo and turn right towards Tavira. On the left at the edge of the town is a large cemetery and the turning to Garcia is 1km after this on the left. Take another turn right signposted to Garcia and park in the village where the surfaced road ends.

A long walk mainly on good tracks and a newly surfaced but traffic-free road. The walk is undulating with a total height gain only about 200m. Distance: 12km. Time: 4hrs. Map: 50A Ameixal and 50B Alcoutim. Grade: Very Easy.

From Garcia walk along the track from the road end and in a couple of minutes look for a good footpath on the left side. Follow this over a col on the right-hand side of a small pinewood. This re-joins the track from Garcia at a junction below three ruined windmills. It is worth making the short diversion uphill to look at these, one of which still has some machinery left inside. Return to the junction and continue along the main track. (The branch right goes only to the small village of Passa Frio.)

After about half an hour a surfaced road is met. Turn right and follow this over a col from which a trig point on Bicudo at 384m

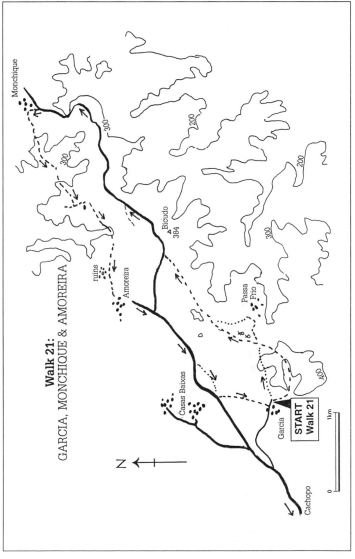

Walk 21:
GARCIA, MONCHIQUE & AMOREIRA

Monchique

300

300

200

200

300

400

Bicudo
384

ruins

Amoreira

Passa
Frio

Casas Baixas

Garcia

**START
Walk 21**

Cachopo

N ←

0   1km

Near Garcia

could be reached in a short diversion through some dense *matos*. Follow this surfaced road on as it swings round in big bends keeping a constant height until the signpost to Monchique is reached. Turn left into the village but turn left again before the first house on to a good cart-track. Ignore a fork right and keep on the uphill track passing what look like one or two haystacks. They are not haystacks, but storage huts constructed of reeds and grasses. At a cross-track take a left turn and continue downhill to cross a stream-bed in the bottom of the valley. After rising up again on the other side a T-junction is met on a ridge. Turn left, passing a large goat-shed with electric fencing on the right. The track soon bends sharp right and goes through an area of almonds, olives, cork oaks and some umbrella pines.

Shortly after passing a stone enclosure with two narrow openings the village of Amoreira is reached. Beyond it the surfaced road is met again. Turn right towards Cachopo and 20 minutes later take a branch track on the left. This is an old track which crosses a stream-bed and rises to re-join the new road. Turn left and 2 minutes later turn left again on an unsurfaced track to return to Garcia in a further 5 minutes.

Garcia to Monchique: 1hr 35mins. Monchique to Amoreira: 1hr 40mins. Amoreira to Garcia: 45mins.

22: ODELEITE

Odeleite is the name of a small town set on a north-east facing hillside and also the name of the attractive stream which winds along the valley below it. The town, or rather a large village, is untouched by time and very typical of the old Algarve with a tangle of old houses between steep and narrow streets. Most of the houses have small gardens or yards with mules or hens or pigs. The stream runs between banks of the giant reeds, or *Arundo donax*, and the rich alluvial soil in the valley floor is intensively cultivated with oranges, almonds and vines. The route is a circular one, crossing the stream by stepping stones before climbing up to the hill-top village of Alcarias. The route then descends to the valley and returns along the bank of the stream. A short diversion can be made to an old mill which has three intact sets of mill wheels in place.

To reach Odeleite from the central Algarve take the new P1 motorway to Castro Marim and turn north on the EN122 towards

Old mill, Odeleite

Mertola. There is a car park at the entrance to the village, although the access point may change when the new *barragem* (under construction in 1993) is completed.

On good tracks all the way, once the stepping stones have been negotiated; these are wide-topped and present no difficulties, but the fast flowing water is intimidating to some. A long cane which can be picked up nearby is a great help in balancing. The total uphill is less than 100m. Distance: 7.5km. Time: 2hrs 50mins. Map: 50B Alcoutim. Grade: Easy.

From the car park walk downhill into the village making towards the church. After passing the post office turn right and go past the church and then left towards the stream. This is crossed by the stepping stones mentioned above. The track continues through an orange grove and then rises up through low hills to join a quiet country road near Alcarias. Turn left and go through the village, then continue along the road for a short distance to the K3 marker

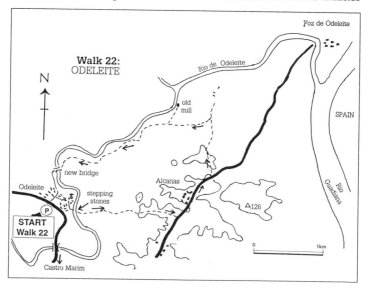

stone. Half a minute later turn left along an earthen track and follow it for about 15 minutes to reach a fork. Turn sharp left here and go down towards some cultivated fields with oranges and almonds with the river beyond. Turn right to reach the ruins of the old mill in about 5 minutes. Return the same way to the track and continue along the bank of the stream to reach the new bridge leading back into Odeleite.

23: AZINHAL AND THE RIO GUADIANA

The village of Azinhal is very typical of the eastern Algarve and as yet untouched by tourism. It lies to the north of Castro Marim on the EN122, one of the main roads running north into the Alentejo region. Between Azinhal and the Rio Guadiana which forms the frontier with Spain is an area of quiet countryside with low rolling hills. There are scattered almond trees and cork oaks among unfenced fields growing legumes and cereals. In between the field are open grassy areas, closely carpeted in spring with the intensely white flowers of chamomile as dazzling as freshly fallen snow in the spring sunshine. Here and there are tiny deep blue irises. The gum cistus in this area does not grow as tall as it does in the west but seems to flower earlier and the large saucer-like white flowers blotched with carmine pink are very attractive.

Down by the river there is a flat area, providing good grazing for sheep and cattle and partly rough marshland. This supports plants that can stand occasional inundation with salt water such as *Ariplex glaucum* which forms sub-shrubs of a reddish colour. The riverside is a good place for birds too. Expect to see many storks flying overhead. Near the start of the walk is an old windmill with much of its mechanism intact and by the river the remains of a frontier guard post.

Approaching Azinhal from the south on the EN122, turn right into the village and drive past the church to the cemetery where there is ample parking.

A very pleasant walk through open country on good tracks with gentle ups and downs, although the riverside track can be slippery after rain. Distance: 10km. Time: 3hrs 30mins. Map: 50D Vila Real de San António. Grade: Very Easy.

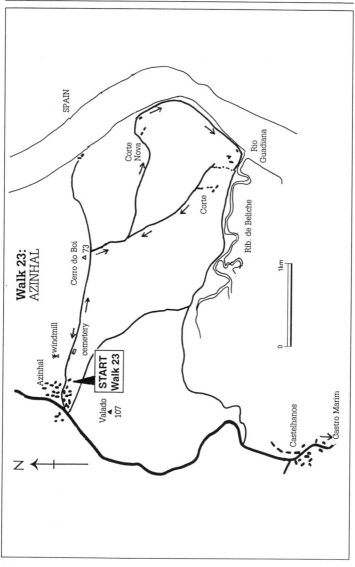

Walk 23:
AZINHAL

SPAIN

Corte Nova

Rio Guadiana

Corte

Rib. de Beliche

Cerro do Boi
▲ 73

windmill

cemetery

START
Walk 23

Azinhal

Valado
▲ 107

1km

0

Castelhanos

Castro Marim

N ←

Walk along the unsurfaced track away from the village and towards the river. After about 20 minutes there is a branch path on the left to the trig point of Cerro do Boi at 73m, worth taking. Return to the track and 200m further on take a right fork. In a further 10 minutes take a left fork. This track continues between low hills and then descends to the river. Ignore a branch path on the right shortly before reaching a farmhouse on the left. On the river bank there is a small landing place and a fiscal guard post.

The track now closely follows the river bank downstream and almost immediately there is an idyllic picnic spot on a rocky outcrop fragrant with wild flowers. The next part of the track continues very close to the river with views across to Spain. The strikingly different marshland vegetation takes over and the track is covered with fine silt. Wet patches may be avoided by walking on the narrow embankment on the left or through the edge of the field on the right. Continue along the river bank towards the ruins of the old frontier post seen on the low hill ahead. Although the track skirts the bottom of this hill it is worth going up it for the fine view.

Continue along the track below the low cliff, turning inland and keeping to the foot of the almond-clad slope. After about 250m a wide track is met. Turn right and follow it up through the almonds, cork oaks and gum cistus. A track comes in from the left and in a further 15 minutes the outward track is joined. Follow this back to the starting point.

Iberian birthwort

WALKING ROUTES
The Coast

The coastal walking in the Algarve must be among the best in Europe, in particular the west Atlantic coast north of Cape St Vincent which is now a protected area. The attractions of these cliff walks are outstanding, but a word of warning is necessary. Cliff edges are potentially dangerous places especially where the rock is very friable and anyone who chooses to walk close to the edge does so entirely at their own risk. Do not be tempted to emulate the local fishermen, who seem to choose the most precarious situations and get away with it. Not all do. Not only are some of the cliff edges friable and eroded, there are deep blowholes where the sea has worn away the lower strata of the cliffs and pushed deep inland. These spectacular holes are come upon without warning and are very deep with vertical or near vertical sides. All the same, provided due care and attention is paid, these walks are some of the most rewarding it is possible to do.

If you are walking on sandy beaches backed by high cliffs remember that this is not the Mediterranean but the Atlantic and tides can be high. Find out locally what the time of low tide is before attempting walks 28 and 35 for example.

Two of the most dangerous places are the cliffs of Praia da Rocha and Praia do Vau, near Portimão. Attempts have been made to patch up the worst places with reinforced cement and parts of the coastal road have been cordoned off. Avoid this area; there are plenty of other places which are perfectly safe provided care is taken.

Further short walks in coastal areas are described in the chapter on Wildlife and Nature Reserves. These include the Alvor estuary and Castro Marim.

Note that distances and times given for these coastal walks can only be approximate. It is possible to take such meandering routes and to spend so long in interesting diversions and in photography that this is not surprising. Photographers are advised to take plenty of film.

24: ESTEVEIRA

Esteveira is a small nature reserve on the Atlantic coast north of Aljezur. It is a dune area and a fragile habitat so that visitors are requested to stay on the existing tracks and paths and to avoid trampling the dune vegetation. The plants in the pre-dune area include aromatic inula, colourful hottentot figs, sage-leaved cistus and the striking endemic Portuguese milk vetch (see p24). On a day in early February the author and party found the endemic thrift *Armeria pungens*, a red oxalis, several yellow rock-roses and the beautiful blue lithospermum and many others. There are outstanding views of the sea and the cliffs and the area is completely unspoilt. Inland there are some cultivated fields and grazing cattle and a few small cottages. There is a trig point at 75m among the pine trees which grow on a knoll in the centre of the area which is bounded by two small streams running in a south-east to north-west direction.

Esteveira is reached by driving north from Aljezur to Rogil. At the northern end of the village turn left along the signposted road and continue to the end of the surfaced road, about 10 minutes' drive in all from Aljezur.

A short walk around the reserve with no significant ups and downs. It can easily be followed by Walk 25. Distance: 2.5km. Time: 1hr 15mins., or longer for serious botanists. Map: 49A Odeciexe. Grade: Very Easy.

Walk along the track on the left which leads to two small houses and continue on towards the sea. On the right is a deep and vegetated ravine. When the track ends at a spring with a large water jar go up the short but steep sandy path on the left to get to the cliff-top. Continue on to a flat shelf overlooking the sea. A small sandy beach lies below and northwards the cliffs stretch as far as Cape Gardão. Turn left to follow the edge of the cliff and reach another terrace with outstanding views. Further on there is a wet area on the cliff edge with some of the giant reeds normally found on river banks, but here they are only about 8ft high. Further south, before reaching

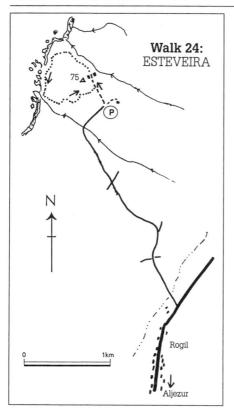

Walk 24:
ESTEVEIRA

the second gully that defines the area, a sloping promontory juts out into the sea. It is worth while descending about half way for the fine views in both directions. To the south is a long beach of white sand. After returning to the cliff-top, it is rewarding to walk over to the edge of the gully before turning inland and picking up the wandering path between the pinewood and the cultivated fields. This leads backs to the path between the car park and the cottages near the starting point.

25: ESPARTAL TO PONTA DA ATALAIA

The cliffs between Espartal and the headland of Ponta da Atalaia to the south are slightly less than 50m high. There are views down to sandy beaches and interesting rock formations with dark-coloured metamorphosed sedimentary rocks thrown up into sharp folds. Other rocks lie horizontally forming a kind of reef off-shore, over which the Atlantic breakers crash and roll. Inland there is a dune area rich in wild flowers including the endemic thrift *Armeria pungens* with tall pink flowers, clumps of the intense blue lithospermum, two kinds of yellow rock rose, orchids and wild

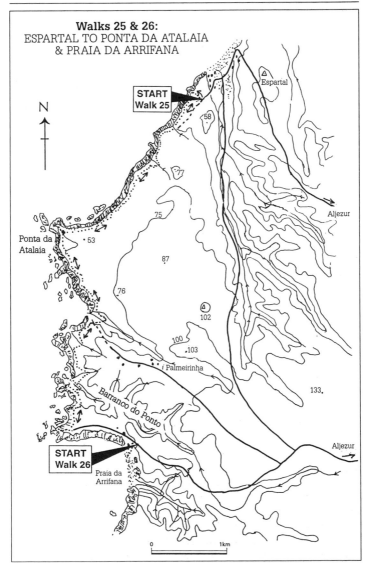

Walks 25 & 26:
ESPARTAL TO PONTA DA ATALAIA
& PRAIA DA ARRIFANA

antirrhinums.

The start of the walk is reached by driving south from Aljezur and taking the first road to the right signposted to Espartal. On the way there are views down into the broad valley of the Aljezur river with some old salt pans. There is a small urbanisation at Espartal where the road descends steeply to the beach and then heads up the cliff on the other side. Park at a junction where a rough track leads towards the cliff. (Fifteen minutes' drive from Aljezur.)

Quite easy walking along sandy trails. Distance: 7km. Time: About 2hrs 20mins. Map: 49A Odeciexe. Grade: Easy.

Leave the drivable fisherman's track to walk south along the cliff edge. There is no path but many meandering trails through the vegetation. Those who want to get down to a long and narrow sandy beach can do so from the turning circle where the fishermen park. Continuing along the cliff it is necessary at one point to go inland because a stream cuts deeply into the cliff. Turn back from the headland of Atalaia, which is the point that can be reached from Arrifana to the south.

26: PRAIA DA ARRIFANA TO PONTA DA ATALAIA

The Praia da Arrifana is a beach of golden sand clean-washed each day by the ocean and enclosed by the encircling arms of steep and rocky cliffs. The cliffs are of metamorphic shales twisted and folded into intricate shapes and there is a detached sea-stack to the south. There are some houses at the back of the beach which is reached by a steep and winding track of granite setts. Although there is some development in the hinterland which has the air of a semi-abandoned urbanisation, this does not detract from the superb cliff scenery. The vegetation on the cliff-top is rather uniform with the endemic *Cistus palinhae* predominating and with gorse, prickly astralagus and aromatic inula. But the cliffs are cut into deeply by several streams where there is a much greater diversity of plants. Prominent on all the north-facing slopes in early February are colonies of a small yellow daffodil, *Narcissus bulbocardium*, the hoop-petticoat narcissus.

The area is approached from Lagos by taking the EN120 to

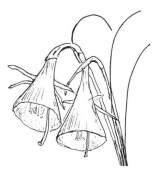

Hoop-petticoat narcissus

Aljezur and turning left 500m before the town on a road signposted to Arrifana. Turn left at a T-junction and then follow the road signs. Park opposite a cafe where the descent to the beach begins.

Quite difficult walking on narrow shale paths with several ups and downs. Distance: 11km. Time: 4hrs. Map: 48D Bordeira. Grade: Difficult.

Before beginning the main walk to the north it is worth going down to the sandy bay and walking to the south along the beach. A sidestream cuts deeply back into the cliff and can be followed inland for some way before the vegetation becomes too dense. This diversion will be of particular interest to botanists, or for anyone who wants to try and find a way up to the prominent obelisk of Arrifana.

Return to the cliff-top by the descent route or by the other road going up behind the boats at the north end of the beach. Follow the road to the headland where there is a ruined fort. Start walking north from the road end and after a short descent take a branch path right leading down into the stream-bed of the Barranco do Ponto. This path leads down to a small pebble beach with many rounded and flattened rocks attractively veined with quartz. To continue, return along the stream-bed past a little waterfall and round a sharp bend to the right. When the stream turns sharp left again go up the spur which leads to the cliff-top at a reasonable angle. (It is possible to scramble up the shale cliff by a more direct line but this is extremely loose and steep and not advised.)

After this follow along the cliff top noting that there are three more streams to cross and in each case this involves a detour inland. After the second of these a turning circle at a track end is crossed. The third stream runs a straight course from south-east to north-west. Before descending to this stream there is a narrow path back inland and parallel to the stream. At this point an unexpected deluge deterred us from continuing to the Ponta da Atalaia and we followed the path back to a large ruined building then headed directly back towards the buildings on the Arrifana headland. This is quite quick but there is a descent through *matos* (quite dense) to cross the Barranco do Ponto. There should be no problems in continuing the walk along the cliff to the Ponta da Atalaia.

27: PONTAL

Pontal is a headland on the Western Atlantic coast with multi-coloured cliffs forming spectacular rock scenery. There are many little bays and headlands and a number of off-shore stacks and rocky islands. There are sand dunes inland on the northern part and the cliffs are limited to the north by the large sandy beach of Praia da Bordeira and to the south by the Praia do Amado. Fishing from the steep rocks, often from very precarious positions, is a popular sport with local people. On Sundays in particular there are dozens of fishermen with families and friends and there are picnics and barbecues all the way along the cliff-tops. Other days it is almost deserted so avoid Sundays if you prefer peace and quiet. Although this headland is now part of the west coast protected area there are several half completed houses near the coast and a number of fishermen's shelters. Some of these are built of reeds in a traditional manner so blend in with the landscape and are not obtrusive.

Access is by three roads from the small village of Carrapateira and they are all linked by a track which follows the cliff-top. From the southern end of the village take the road to Praia do Amado where there is ample parking.

Easy walking along the cliff edge and very easy along the return route. Distance: 10km. Time: About 4hrs. Map: 48D Bordeira. Grade: Easy.

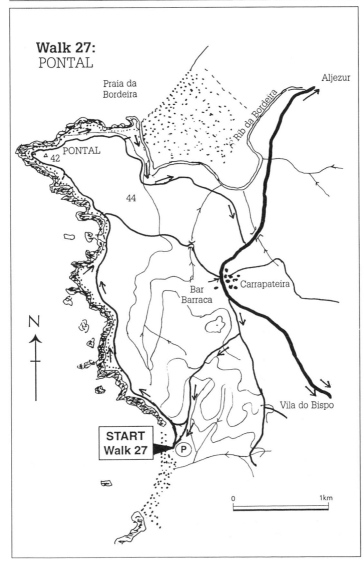

Walk 27:
PONTAL

Praia da
Bordeira

Aljezur

Rib da Bordeira

PONTAL

△ 42

44

Bar
Barraca

Carrapateira

N

Vila do Bispo

**START
Walk 27**

P

0   1km

Begin by walking north up the cliff road, leaving it as soon as practicable in favour of the cliff edge. After about 15 minutes' there is a road down to a little harbour for small boats, with a café up above on the cliff top. (This may be closed in winter.) At one point on the edge of a vertical cliff there is a large tripod supporting a pulley, possibly for hauling up catches before the access road to the harbour was made. All the way there are constantly changing views of the sea and the cliffs. Further on there is another small bay where colourful fishing boats are hauled out above a slipway, with an access road leading part way down. This is where the reed shelters are and beside them there is a sloping promontory which makes a very good viewpoint.

Beyond this is a long stretch of fairly unbroken cliff before the trig point of Pontal (42m) comes into sight. The headland forms a distinct point here with another promontory sloping out into the sea. It is one of the favourite spots for fishing. After this point the coastline turns to the east and the cliffs diminish in height towards the Bordeira beach. There are some large dunes here and paths can be followed over these with views down to the Bordeira beach where the river leaves large pools that attract wading birds. Join the road inland and walk through Carrapateira to return to the starting point.

An alternative is to return by the rough but drivable track just inland from the cliff edge, to continue enjoying the views of the sea. This is much quicker walking than following the cliff-edge path.

28: PRAIA DO CASTELEJO

This long strip of sandy beach is north-west of Vila do Bispo, an attractive village north of Sagres. There are many small islands and sea-stacks against which the Atlantic breakers crash sending up impressively high plumes of spray. The cliffs backing the beach are not as steep as some on this coast but are composed of interesting layers of highly-folded strata. This short walk can only be done at low tide as the beach is completely covered when the tide is right in. The cliff-top is shale and sparsely vegetated, with low prostrate forms of juniper, rosemary and the endemic *Cistus palinhae* all in mat or cushion like formations. On the north facing slopes grow large colonies of the tiny *Narcissus bulbocardium* and on the cliff-top

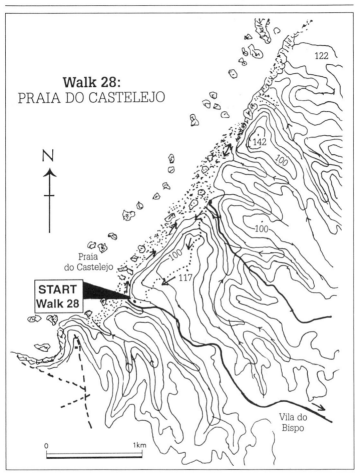

prostrate forms of acacia were observed. The views from the clifftop are excellent. At low tide and only at low tide the walk can be extended northward along the deserted beach.

Approaching from Vila do Bispo find the signposted road at the west side of the village and park at the road end at Praia do Castelejo.

Easy walking along the shore, a moderate pull up a shaly cliff path to the top and a fairly gradual descent on pathless but easy ground. Distance: 3km. Time: 1hr. Map: 51B Vila do Bispo. Grade: Moderate.

Walk north-east along the sand for about 25 minutes to reach a beach bar (closed in winter) at the end of another access road. Go up the shaly cliff to the south by an erosion channel which is almost like a path. The top is reached in about 15 minutes. Follow the cliff edge downwards to return to the starting point. Further down the cliff there is more vegetation among which are large cushion-shaped clumps of *Astralagus massiliensis*. This has small white flowers and looks attractive but is extremely prickly.

29: PONTA RUIVA AND TORRE DE ASPA

Ponta Ruiva is a striking red rocky point on the coast west of Vila do Bispo. There is a sandy beach behind it virtually inaccessible by car: only local fishermen risk their cars on the rough tracks. The Torre de Aspa is no historic tower but a geodesic obelisk about 10m high erected in 1959 for surveying purposes. On the highest point of the flat tableland behind the cliffs at 156m it can be seen for miles and makes a splendid viewpoint. A little further to the north past an abandoned customs building is a viewpoint on the edge of the cliffs looking down on to the Praia do Castelejo, the scene of Walk 28. To the south, the walk overlaps slightly with Walk 30.

The walk is started from Vale Santo and this can be reached either by taking the first right after Vila do Bispo and driving on a rough track for 8km or making a longer drive round by Sagres and turning right from the road to the Cape.

Easy walking on wide tracks. Walking on the cliff edge is possible in places, but there is hardly any path as such and it is not recommended. Distance: 16km. Time: About 4hrs. Map: 51B Vila do Bispo. Grade: Easy. (Walking on the cliff edge between A and B, shown on the sketch map, is Difficult.)

From Vale Santo walk north along the rough track, turning right on

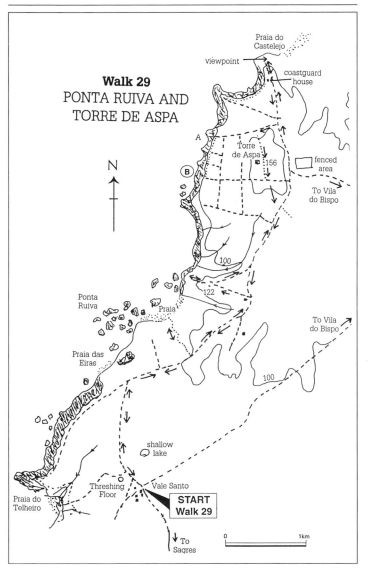

Walk 29
PONTA RUIVA AND
TORRE DE ASPA

Praia do
Castelejo

viewpoint

coastguard
house

N

A

Torre
de Aspa

◼ 156

fenced
area

To Vila
do Bispo

B

100

122

Ponta
Ruiva

Praia

To Vila
do Bispo

Praia das
Eiras

100

shallow
lake

Praia do
Telheiro

Threshing
Floor

Vale Santo

**START
Walk 29**

↓ To
Sagres

0   1km

127

joining another track in about 20 minutes. There is a small beach, the Praia das Eiras, down on the left. A branch track on the left leads to a viewpoint on the headland directly behind the red rock and a few minutes later the branch path down to the Praia da Ponta Ruiva is reached. Returning from the beach continue along the track in the same direction as before. After passing another track coming in on the right take the left turn just past an old building and follow the track out to where it ends on the headland past the 122 marker stone. The views are very fine from here. Turning inland again take the left fork to return to the main track north. Follow this on to the old coastguard station, passing to the right of the obelisk. Another track joins in near a fenced area. (This comes from Vila do Bispo and can be used as a walk into the area by walkers using public transport. See note at end.)

Return the same way, taking the second right turn and then first left to reach the Torre. After this, either cut across south to join the main track and follow this back to Vale Santo, or go back north and then left out to the road end to walk along the cliff edge between A and B. The cliff-top north of A is vegetated and in places impossible; south of B is an unstable area with landslips, crumbling edges and holes and cracks in the ground. Between A and B there are two gullies which must be crossed and it is quite pleasant and interesting. After this return to the main track south.

Note: To reach the area from Vila do Bispo, take the road past the shop on the western outskirts of the village. After passing a football field take the second track on the left and keep going past a few small houses to join the track near the obelisk by the fenced area. This is about 4km.

30: CABO DE SÃO VICENTE (CAPE SAINT VINCENT)

Cabo de São Vicente is still known as the *Fim do Mondo* or 'End of the world', the name given it before the voyages of exploration in the fifteenth century. It is the most westerly part of the European continent and the early Portuguese explorers who first ventured to sail down the coast of Africa to find the sea route to India, to reach the spice islands and to explore the north Atlantic all set sail from either Lisbon or Sagres. The cape was their last sight of the known

Between Burgau and Salema (Walk 32)
Praia de Martinhal, near Sagres (Walk 31)

Luz (Walk 33)
Chapel of Nossa Senhora da Rocha (Walk 34)

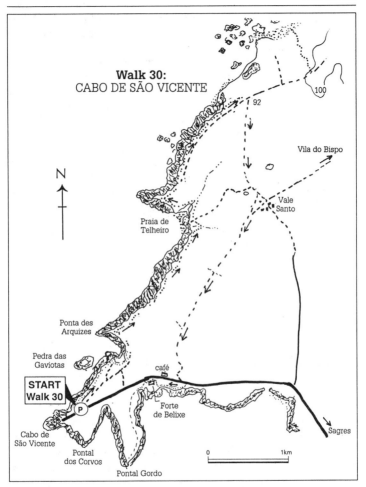

Walk 30:
CABO DE SÃO VICENTE

world. There is a lighthouse which is sometimes open to the public, with an observation platform reached by 73 steps up a spiral staircase. (Opening hours depend on availability of keepers, but there is also a lookout place on the cliff-top.) From here the shipping on the main route between the Atlantic and the Mediterranean can be watched and in spring and autumn it is a good place for migrating birds. The area is of great interest both for the cliff scenery and for the wild flowers, some of which are unique to this area. The area of the cape itself is topped by a limestone pavement on which grow endemic forms of thrift and of cistus. *Armeria pungens* forms clumps of very tall pink fowers, normally in April and May but some may be found as early as February. *Cistus palinhae* is a dwarf type of gum cistus which has dark green shiny leaves which are extremely sticky and white crinkly flowers without the pink spot of *Cistus ladanifer*. In early December we found carpets of bright white alyssum everwhere and many clumps of the yellow-flowered daisy *Asteriscus maritimus*.

Further north along the coast the limestone gives way to shales and all the way to the Ponta de Telheiro there are impressive views of the cliffs and sea-stacks. Fishermen may be seen in some exciting situations. The return route slightly inland is a complete contrast, on a flat grassy plain where cattle graze and flocks of birds wheel overhead. We saw thekla larks, meadow pipits, jackdaws, Sardinian warblers and black redstarts but failed to spot the stone curlews and little bustards which others have seen here. This was early December and we saw no-one except fishermen on the rocks near the cape and scuba divers on the small beach at Telheiro.

Very rough walking as far as Telheiro. After this it becomes easier and the return is very easy along a good track. Distance: 12km. Time: Allow about 5hrs. Map: 51B Vila do Bispo. Grade: Difficult.

Follow the cliff edge northwards. A large sea-stack, the Pedra das Gaviotas or 'Seagull rock', lies off-shore just before reaching a little bay. It is worth descending the sloping ground at the south side of the bay for a close view of the rock which is connected to the land by a natural rock bridge, under which the sea rushes noisily. On the way up again to the cliff-top a tiny sandy beach is seen below a steeply overhanging cliff. Following the cliff edge to the north of this little bay another headland is reached, the Ponta des Arquizes. After this the coastline runs a straighter course until the Praia de Telheiro is reached. Two streams here involve slight diversions inland. In between the streams a rough sandy track used by fishermen is crossed. Keep following the cliff-top to reach the headland of the Ponta de Telheiro in a further 20 minutes.

After this the cliff-top walking becomes easier and strong walkers may be tempted to continue to the Praia do Pedra Ruiva, the Beach of the Red Rock. I recommend saving that for another day and being content with reaching the viewpoint from the headland over the Praia das Eiras. Return to the track junction and follow the wide track which runs almost due south to Vale Santo. After about 20 minutes a branch track leads to Telheiro. Nearby is a large threshing floor and the track leading to the fort of Beliche near the lighthouse begins here, bypassing the cluster of buildings at Vale Santo.

When the main Sagres road is met opposite a sign saying '5km Sagres, 1km Cap St Vincent' turn left then immediately right for an enjoyable cliff-top path leading to the fort. After this it is best to re-join the road to return to the starting point. Following the cliff edge around Pontal Gordo is not recommended as there is no path and the going is very rough.

31: FIGUEIRA TO SAGRES
(The full walk is Nos. 33, 32, 31 together)

This is the longest of the three stages of the walk from Lagos to Sagres and is difficult to shorten because the main road is some distance from the sea. Shorter sections can only be walked by using a car, for example to reach Ingrina. This walk is quite varied with cliff-top sections and several descents to sandy beaches, ending with a walk along the long beach of Martinhal where it makes a refreshing change to take the boots off and walk along in the edge of the sea. There is a small harbour at Sagres and several convenient bars near the bus terminus, but Sagres itself is worth further exploration on another day.

Although the walking is mainly easy, there are some rough paths and care must be taken with cliff edges and several blowholes. Distance: 16km. Time: Allow about 6hrs. Maps: 51B Vila do Bispo (mainly) and 52A Portimão. Grade: Moderate.

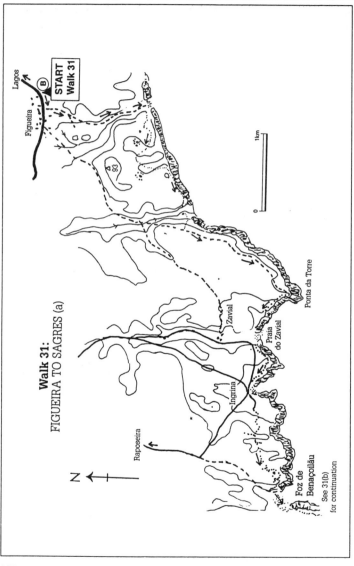

Walk 31:
FIGUEIRA TO SAGRES (a)

N

START
Walk 31

Lagos

Figueira

93

1km

Ponta da Torre

Zavial

Praia
do Zavial

Ingrina

Raposeira

Foz de
Benaçoilâu

See 31(b)
for continuation

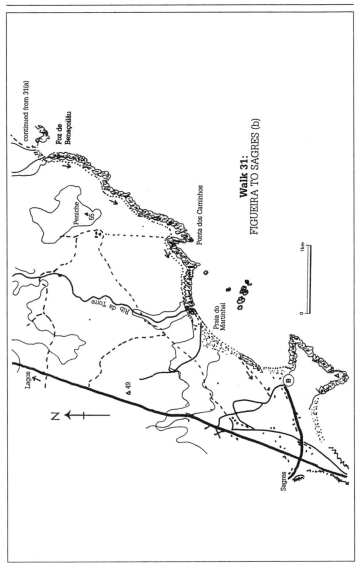

continued from 31(a)

Foz de
Benaçoliâu

Peniche
▲ 55

Ponta dos Caminhos

Rib de Torre

Praia do
Martinhal

Lagos ↑

▲ 49

N ←

Sagres

Walk 31:
FIGUEIRA TO SAGRES (b)

B

0   1km

From the bus stop in Figueira walk downhill on the main road for a couple of minutes and then turn left into the Rua de Rossio. When the road ends go straight on along the unsurfaced track ahead towards the coast. When it bends right near the fenced area of the water treatment plant turn left along a red earth path. The track leads to a small beach through a narrow partly cultivated valley. As the coast is approached there are some crags high up on the right-hand side where we saw numerous pigeons taking flight and landing again. We had a tantalising glimpse of two birds of prey up above, probably buzzards.

From the beach there is a steep pull up a stony trod leading to a flat top. There are many small pine trees and in late autumn tall dead stalks of fennel. After reaching a track in a valley bottom a cairn marks the continuation of the path back uphill again. The path changes direction several times, then crosses another little valley and passes an old cultivated area. Look out for a large pile of stones on a boulder to indicate where the path goes downhill a little. This is the only section of the walk where the walking is really rather rough with loose stones and scree. Two small sandy bays are seen below. At the second one it is necessary to climb up rough ground to avoid a steeper section of loose cliff. Soon the descent to the second Figueira beach begins. The stony path heads down a ridge and when this steepens above some caves, a way down to the beach can be found on the right.

Cross the beach and follow a rough path up to the cliff-top again, passing a strange ruined building with a tiled floor. Turn left along a wide earth-track leading south. A more major track is met and followed on to the Ponta de Torre where there is a sudden surprise view of the bay of Zavial where we saw the sea full of surfers waiting for the Atlantic rollers to sweep them to the beach. A few minutes' descent leads down to the sandy beach, where it is best to walk along the sand. At the beach café turn up steeply towards a new house and then follow the obvious track to Ingrina. Turn left on the road and five minutes later a road junction with an engraved stone marker is met. Go up the wide track which meanders upwards parallel to the coast. Ignore a branch inland and when the track levels off follow it to the left. Turn left at a T-junction to reach a ruin. Follow the path below down to the wide beach of Foz de Benaçoilāu.

Cross the beach and follow the path to the top of the cliff again. The next section is fairly level but paths meander here and there and sometimes inland detours are needed to avoid vegetation. Look out for an occasional blowhole as the point of Ponta dos Caminhos is reached. Cut across this point if preferred, then pick up the cliff path again at the head of a deep inlet. There are views of several small islands in the bay of Martinhal. Before reaching the bay there is a descent to cross a river by a bar of boulders. Then a final pull up over a small cliff and down to the sandy beach. At the far end a wide track rises easily to reach the houses. Turn left to get to the bus stop.

32: BURGAU TO FIGUEIRA

This is the second stage of the walk from Lagos to Sagres and is the shortest, allowing time for relaxing on a beach or in the attractive village of Salema. The highlights include the Ponta de Almadena and the sudden view of a small sandy bay below, not shown on the map. There is also an old fort, built by the Spanish when they occupied the country in 1660. In spite of extensive damage in the 1755 earthquake some substantial walls remain and it is in a splendid situation on the edge of the cliffs.

Mostly easy walking, but take the usual care on cliff edges. Distance: 10km. Time: About 4hrs. Map: 52A Portimão. Grade: Moderate.

From Burgau there is no direct way from the beach to the cliff-top so from the corner by the bus stop take the road to the west. Just out of the village turn left on to a footpath by a red lozenge sign (which means it is an area where hunting is not allowed). There are fig trees inland and a view across to the Monchique hills. The path goes downhill to a flattish area then continues to the Ponta de Almadena. Either keep to the cliff edge for the best views or join a wider track slightly inland for easier walking. From the point follow a narrow path down past a ruined building and heading inland. When a wider track is met, turn left to descend to the beach where there is a café. The path back to the cliff-top begins right at the side of this café and is a little steep at first. A little further on a new villa has been built and unfortunately allowed to annexe part of the cliff path. It is

135

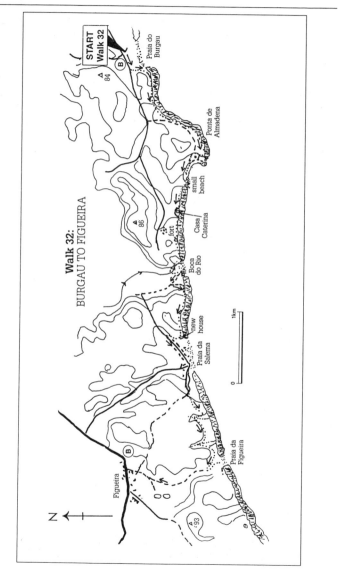

Walk 32:
BURGAU TO FIGUEIRA

START
Walk 32

Praia do Burgau

△ 84

Ponta de Almadena

small beach

△ 86

Casa Caterina

fort

Boca do Rio

new house

Praia da Salema

1km

0

Figueira

Praia da Figueira

N ←

△ 93

necessary to descend alongside the fence to join the track to the house and turn left. The path continues after crossing a little gully and soon reaches the ruins of the fort on the very edge of the cliff.

Beyond the fort the path descends to a flat valley and small beach, the Boca do Rio. Follow the path in a slight detour inland to cross the river by a narrow bridge. The fenced off area protects some Roman remains which have yet to be excavated. Turn right inland then double back left to return to the cliff-top. Continue along the top until another new house forces a diversion inland leading to a long narrow street of old houses, the Rua dos Pescadores. This leads down into Salema, a pleasant village with fishing boats and several bars. Buses return to Lagos from here if anyone wants to shorten the walk.

Continue the walk by taking the old cobbled track leading uphill. Join the road winding up between the new houses on the left. When the road ends a track continues straight on and then descends into a narrow valley with a path going back inland. Ignore a branch track doubling back right and 2 minutes later leave the main track and return towards the sea again. Five minutes later take a right fork, then vee into a narrow gully where one path goes inland and a fisherman's path goes down to the sea. Five minutes later the attractive sandy beach of Figueira is seen below and a good path followed down and inland. This narrow valley is partly cultivated and we noticed two wells. When the track widens and bends right two ponds are seen on the left; part of a water treatment plant for Vila do Bispo. Join the wider track from this place and turn right, to reach the outskirts of the village. Ignore a left branch and walk up the Rua de Rossio to reach the main road. Turn right uphill towards the telephone box to find the bus stop.

33: LAGOS TO BURGAU

Every part of the coast between Lagos and Sagres can be walked in three days using Lagos as a centre and making use of public transport. This walk descibes the first section. Between Lagos and Burgau the coast is extremely attractive in spite of the degree of development inland and the occasional intrusion of a villa or two on the coast itself. The first part of the walk along the broad walkway by the river with its colourful boats is succeeded by a

Fishing boats near Lagos

cliff-top walk with views of fantastic off-shore rock formations. The cliffs are of mixed and unconsolidated sediments that are crumbling and highly eroded. The paths wind in and out of gullies and out to little headlands all the way to the Ponta da Piedade. At Praia da Mós the cliffs change to a pale cream coloured limestone in fairly regular layers. The descent into Luz sees different scenery again, with views down to a flat valley where cattle graze and large numbers of egrets gather. After Luz the cliff scenery changes again with bands of different sedimentary rocks. Burgau where this walk ends is a pretty place and there are bars and cafés that can occupy the time while waiting for a bus back to Lagos.

Several ups and downs, sometimes fairly rough but mainly easy. Be wary of cliff edges. Distance: 15.5km. Time: Allow 5hrs 30mins. Map: 52A Portimão. Grade: Moderate.

From the bus station in Lagos, or the railway station which is on the opposite side of the river, begin walking along the sea-front which is wide and pleasant. Near a small harbour opposite the old fort the road starts to climb uphill. Opposite the fire station turn left, passing

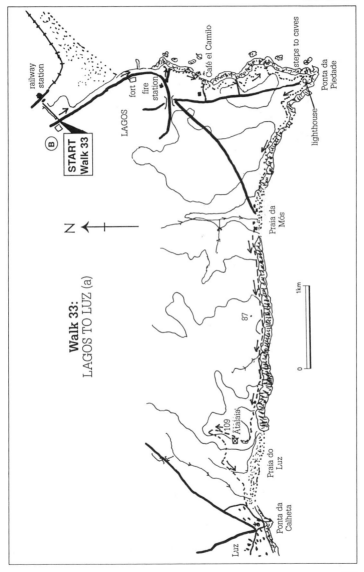

Walk 33:
LAGOS TO LUZ (a)

railway station

LAGOS

START Walk 33

Ⓑ

Café el Camilo

steps to caves

fort

fire station

Ponta da Piedade

lighthouse

Praia da Mós

N

87

109
Atalaia

Praia do Luz

0   1km

Ponta da Calheta

Luz

a 'No through road' sign and then a sign saying 'Praia de Pinho 50m'. At the road-end turn right and follow the cliff-top path. At a T-junction, turn left, the path being paved here. At a road-end near the Golfinho hotel, the continuing path is highly eroded; best to walk along towards the hotel and go up the easier path that begins behind the bus stop.

The cliff-top now is fairly flat grassland with small trees and shrubs housing a number of small birds such as Sardinian warblers and stonechats. To avoid dipping into the numerous gullies which cut back inland a winding course is followed to reach the lighthouse on the Ponta da Piedade. An arrow on the left shows the way to the point across a small bridge. A flight of steps leads down to some caves (which can also be reached by boat from Lagos). The off-shore stacks here are used as breeding grounds by cattle egrets, a most unusual occurrence. Continue along the cliff top to Praia da Mós. After passing a cliff-top campsite there are two flights of steps leading down to a beach café. The top of a little gully with more steps down is passed, before reaching a fenced area with new villas.

At Praia da Mós there are several beach cafés and some public toilets, but these were found to be locked up in November so are probably only open in season. The path up the next section is really a rough 4WD track giving easy walking. As Luz is approached the path diverts inland to reach a large prominent obelisk on the edge

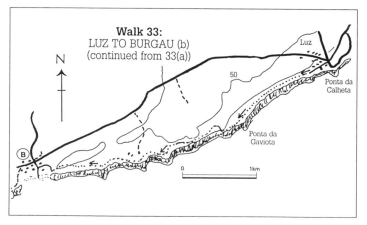

Luz

of some steep ground. There is a path going straight down but it is easier to continue along the top to a ruined farm, then go left and double back below it. There is a short steep bit then an easy but eroded path. After passing a new villa, the Casa Vistamar, a wide track with old stone setts is followed down into Luz.

On reaching Luz turn inland to reach the church. This is where the bus stop is, if a shorter walk is wanted. Turn left in the square by the church to continue the walk. Before passing the last of the houses the track narrows and local fishermen will be seen on the rocks below. There is a good view back of the cream-coloured cliffs, interrupted by dark grey shales. At the edge of a little bay the path turns inland. After crossing a little valley planted with vines, go up and over the hill ahead as the inland path leads to some ploughed fields. At Burgau head inland to find the bus stop.

34: BENAGIL

The coast between Benagil and the chapel of Senhora de Rocha is almost unspoilt and gives one of the most beautiful walks in the Algarve. This is despite the fact that at the end of the walk blocks of villas are seen on the outskirts of Armacão de Pera. The rugged cliffs are layered in bands of cream and ochre sedimentary rocks with one of hard grey shelly limestone forming the cliff-top. There are several sea-stacks, sandy bays, rock arches and spectacular blowholes

Rock arch near Benagil

where the sea can be seen below quite a distance back from the edge of the cliffs. The cliff-tops have numerous wild flowers and shrubs providing cover for many small birds. The opportunities for birdwatching, botanising, photography and simply looking at the fantastic rock formations make this a walk to be taken slowly.

To reach Benagil from the west, turn right at the crossroads by the International School 3km east of Lagoa on the N125. If coming from the east, turning left at this crossroads is not allowed, so drive to the end of the school grounds where there is a signposted place to make a U-turn. There is a small signpost immediately at the crossroads with the names of four beaches, Benagil at the top. After this, follow the signposts. Park by the café at the top of the hill in Benagil, a good place for a drink at the end of the walk and we found it open in late November.

A fairly easy walk except for crossing two deep inlets where the right path must be found. Great care must be taken to watch out for blowholes of which there are many, some obvious but some partly obscured by shrubs. Distance: 11km. Time: Allow a good 4hrs. It takes much longer to follow the cliff edge closely and the return route can be shortened by cutting across inland paths in places. Map: 52B Albufeira. Grade: Moderate.

Start by going towards the sea and by the first house, which is a post office, go up the steps at the side. At the top go right towards the sea, the first headland giving a view back down to the beach at Benagil. The colourful boats are really the only signs that this was once an attractive fishing village, as the old cottages are ruinous and new villas are intruding. Turn away and begin the walk east and it is not long before the first blowhole is seen at the head of a small inlet. All the way from now on the scenery is so eye-catching that it can take a long time covering the first stretch to the car park on the cliff-top at Praia da Marinha. From the corner of this car park a stepped path continues along the cliff-top, with a branch path right going down to the beach. The cliff path rises again and crosses a bridge over a gully to round a corner where some steps and a branch path head inland. A large blowhole is passed and another is skirted just outside a large fenced area, where wild leeks grow in profusion on the cliff-top.

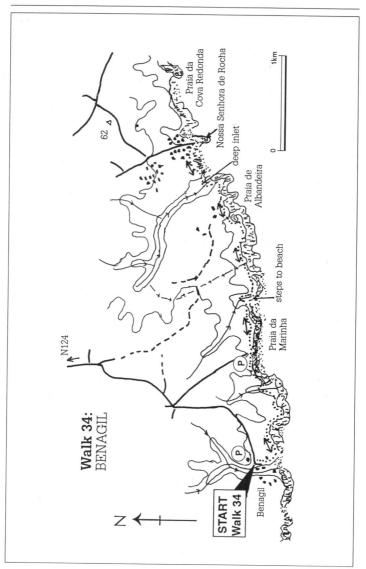

Walk 34:
BENAGIL

Shortly afterwards a shallow valley is crossed, opposite a small rocky island. Five minutes later another inlet is reached where it is necessary to go inland about 100m to find an easy place to descend. Further on at the inlet of Praia de Albandeira there is a small sandy beach and a café-bar, which can be reached by a rough but drivable track. Go up the steps and continue along the cliff-top which becomes deeply indented with rocky ridges stretching out to sea. There are views ahead of an intriguing rocky island, shaped like a tall battleship. More blowholes are seen. After a final headland the coastal path turns inland again to reach a particularly deep but narrow inlet. Follow the path and either take the first branch heading down which is rather difficult at the bottom, or preferably stay on the higher path which leads more easily right to the back of the little beach. Walk towards the sea and after about 100m turn left up a rather scrambly path back up on the cliff. There is a confusion of paths here and one tempting branch to the right is a dead end. Once on the top there is a good path round to the final destination, the white-painted chapel of Nossa Senhora da Rocha on a prominent headland. There are small sandy beaches on either side, but inland it is villa and hotel-land, so this is an appropriate place to end the walk and return to Benagil.

'Battleship' rock

145

35: OLHOS DE ÁGUA TO ALBUFEIRA

Although this part of the coast has become rather built up, this is still a worthwhile walk because of the cliffs and interesting rock formations with isolated stacks and arches, blowholes and caves. It is essential to start the walk about 2 hours before low tide; at high tide it cannot be done. If preferred some of the rocky sections on the foreshore can be avoided by getting up on to a cliff path.

Mainly easy walking but the rocks on the shore are slippery in places. Distance: 11km. Time: About 4hrs. Map: 52B Albufeira. Grade: Moderate.

From the beach at Olhos (see p12) start walking along the sand towards Albufeira, then cross some rocks below a low cliff. After rounding a point where there is a raised rock shelf the walking is on sand again. Some steps up to the cliff-top are passed. About 20 minutes later the white sandy beach of Maria Luisa is reached, with hotels behind. After crossing the beach a square concrete tower with a rope dangling towards the beach is seen. An escape route if caught by the incoming tide?

After crossing some slippery rocks more sand is found, followed by mixed rock and sand and then another large beach, Praia da

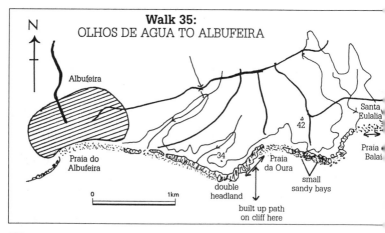

Walk 35:
OLHOS DE AGUA TO ALBUFEIRA

N

Albufeira

Santa Eulalia

Praia Balai

42

Praia do Albufeira

34

Praia da Oura

double headland

small sandy bays

0   1km

built up path on cliff here

Balaia (or Santa Eulalia). There are some concrete steps up and notices warning people not to climb on the cliffs. Ten minutes later there is another beach and 10 minutes further another small sandy bay. Rounding a corner there is a long strip of sand with ice-cream vans and large apartment blocks behind. This is Praia da Oura. A few minutes later, progress on the shore is difficult and it is best to get up on to the cliff path, which here is man-made with bridges over little ravines and steps cut in the rock. Around the corner is another little bay with a sign saying 'Bar open, hot soup, 30m'. Ten minutes later after rounding a final corner, Albufeira comes into sight. Concrete steps lead down to the beach if you want to continue. Our personal choice was to turn back at this point, where there is a double headland with deep circular blowholes.

Return by the same way. Although there is a cliff-top path in places, it is not possible to follow it all the way without trespassing in the grounds of a hotel where a notice at the bottom of the steps says 'For hotel residents only'. Although if you are walking from west to east this notice is not seen until the bottom of the steps to the beach is reached! Also, although parts of it were being repaired in January 1993, in other places paths come to a sudden end at the edge of a steep cliff, a potentially dangerous situation.

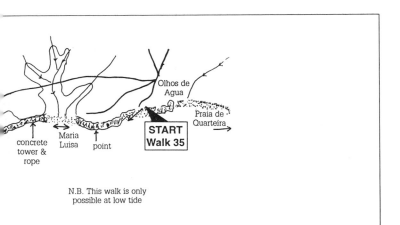

N.B. This walk is only possible at low tide

Golden Wattle

APPENDIX A: LANGUAGE

Anyone familiar with other European languages such as French, Italian and especially Spanish will be able to comprehend some written Portuguese. However, speaking and understanding the spoken word is another matter entirely. Many vowels are nasalised and most 's' sounds are 'shushed' so there is a very different quality to the language which takes some getting used to. The nasalised vowel sounds are indicated by a tilde as in *não*, the word for no. This is pronounced somewhere between 'no' and 'now' when the nostrils are pinched together. Words ending in n or m are pronounced as though there is a 'g' on the end. For example *bom dia* (good morning) sounds a bit like 'bong dia' but without the 'g' being pronounced. An 's' at the beginning of a word is pronounced as in 'soft' but elsewhere as 'sh'. *Sou ingles* (I am English) is pronounced 'soh inglaysh'.

All this sounds very difficult and so it is, but it is well worth taking the trouble to learn to speak a few words. Although hotel staff normally speak English and shopping can usually be achieved by gestures, most people met with while walking in the country only speak Portuguese. They are very friendly people, extremely keen to communicate and always delighted if you can speak a few words of their language.

The best way to learn is directly from a native speaker. In the absence of this possibility, listening to a taped langauge course is very helpful. The linguaphone Travellers' Portuguese can be recommended. Phrase books which do not show the pronunciation are not a great deal of use.

On the whole Portuguese people use language more formally than English people. Always address a stranger as *senhor* or *senhora* (ser-nyor or ser-nyor-rer) and use the basic polite expressions whenever appropriate. (See glossary.)

USEFUL WORDS AND PHRASES

Ten essentials

yes/no	sim/não	seen/now
hello	olá	oh-lah
good morning	bom dia	bon dee-er
good afternoon	boa tarde	boh-er tahr-d
good night	boa noite	boh-er noy-t
please	faz favor	fahsh fer-vohr
thank you	obrigado (for a man)	oh-bree-gah-doo
	obrigada (woman)	oh-bree-gah-der
thank you very much	muito obrigado/a doo/der	mween-to oh-bree-gah-
I'm sorry	desculpe-me	day-sculp-ay-m
I don't understand	não entendo	now en-ten-doh

More basics

do you speak English?	fala ingles?	fah-ler in-glaysh?
please write it down	escreva, faz favor	ish-kray-ver fahsh fer-vohr
can you help me?	pode ajudar-me?	po-d er-zhoo-dahr-m
I don't know	não sei	now say
where are the toilets?	onde são os lavabos?	on-d sow oosh ler-vah-boosh
I'd like/we'd like	queria/queríamos	ker-ree-er/ker-ay-mos
what's that?	o que é isso?	oo ker eh ee-soo
how much is it?	quanto custa?	kwan-to koosh-ter
do you have?	tem?	tayn?
that's fine	está bem	ish-tah baym

Finding your way

where is...?	onde é...?	on-deh
the bus stop	a paragem	ah pah-rah-jeeng
the footpath to..?	a caminho para..?	ah cam-een-yoh pah-rah
the road to..?	a estrada para..?	ah ish-trah-dah pah-rah
is it far?	é longe?	eh lon-zher?
can you show me on this map?	pode indicar-me aqui no mapa?	po-din-dee-kahr-mer-kee noo mah-per

straight ahead	sempre em frente	sen-prayn fren-t
to the left	a esquerda	ah ish-kayr-der
to the right	a direita	ah dee-ray-ter
first/second/third	primeiro/segundo/ terceiro	preem-ay-roo/sergoong- doo/ter-say-roo
here/there	aqui/ali	ah-kee/ah-lee
above/below	em cima/em baixo	eng see-mah/eng bigh-joh
behind/in front	atras/em frente	ah-trahsh/ayn-fren-t

Car travel

I'd like to hire a car	queria alugar um carro	ker-ree-er er-loo-gahr oo kah-rroo
for a day/two days	por um dia/dois dias	por oo deer/dohysh deers
for a week	por uma semana	por oo-mer ser-mer-ner
what is the charge?	qual e a tarifa?	koo-ahl eh er ter-ree-fer
comprehensive insurance	seguro contra todos os riscos	ser-goo-roo kon-trer toh-doosh oosh rish-koosh
can I park here?	posso estacionar aqui?	possoo ishterr-syoonahr er-kee
petrol station/garage	estacao de servicio/ garagem	ish-ter-sow der serr-vee- soo/ger-rah-zhayn
20 litres of super	vinte litros de super	vint lee-troosh der soo pehr
30 litres of regular	trinta litros de normal	trint lee-troosh der normahl
fill it up please	encha, faz favor	ayn-sher fahsh fer-vohr

APPENDIX B: READING LIST

Anderson, Brian and Anderson, Eileen *Landscapes of Portugal* (Algarve). Sunflower Books, 1991

Cook, Thomas *Travellers Algarve* AA Publishing, 1993

Crawshaw, Gerry *Essential Algarve and southern Portugal* Automobile Association, 1981

Davis, Paul & Gibbons, Bob *Field guide to wild flowers of southern Europe* Crowood Press, 1993

Heinzel, H., Fitter, R. and Parslow, J. *The birds of Britain and Europe* Collins, 1972

Kaplon, Marion *The Portuguese: the land and its people* Penguin, 1991

Mabberley, D.P. and Placito, P.J. *Algarve plants and landscape* Oxford U.P., 1993

Peterson, R., Mountfort, G and Hollom, P.A.D. *A field guide to the birds of Britain and Europe* Collins, 4th ed. 1983

Polunin, Oleg & Huxley, Anthony *Flowers of the Mediterranean* Chatto, 1981

Rocha Afonso, Maria da Luz *Plantas do Algarve* with illus. by Mary McMurtrie, Portugal, 1991

Schonfelder, Ingrid & Schonfelder, Peter *Collins photoguide to the wildflowers of the Mediterranean* Collins, 1984

Wuerpel, Charles *The Algarve province of Portugal* David & Charles, 1974 (o.p.)

APPENDIX C: USEFUL INFORMATION A to Z

Banks:
Opening hours 08.30-11.45, 13.00-14.45 Mon. to Fri. Closed Sat. and Sun.

Car hire:
In December 1993 the cost of hiring a small car was typically 9,000$00 for 3 days, 18,000$00 for 7 days. Sometimes you see cheaper prices advertised, but check that these include CDW (collision damage waiver). For walking groups, a Ford Transit seating 9 cost 30,000$00 for 3 days and 60,000$00 for 7 days. To hire a car you must be over 21, have a full driving licence and show your passport.

Premier Car Hire of Harlow have always proved reliable.
Tel: 01279 641040.

Chemists:
Farmacias are open during normal shopping hours and in larger resorts one is on duty 24 hours.

Currency:
The rate of exchange in 1993 was just under 250 *escudos* to the pound. Most hotels change money but sometimes ask for a high commission.

Driving:
Accident records on the main roads are high and dangerous overtaking is common. Impatient drivers try to force slower cars on to the inner lane which is meant for really slow traffic such as donkey carts. Use of seat belts is compulsory and on-the-spot fines for non-use and other offences is high. Driving licence and documents must be carried at all times. Speed limits are:

    motorways, 120kms per hour
    main roads, 90kms per hour
    built up areas, 60kms per hour
    towns, 40kms per hour
(See also Car hire).

Emergencies:
For all emergency services dial 115 and ask for: *policia, bombeiros* (fire service) or *ambulancia*.

Festivals:
Official public holidays are as follows:
1 January, Shrove Tuesday (variable), 25 April, 1 May, 10 June, 15 August, 5 October, 1 November, 8 December and 25 December.

Markets:
Open Mon. to Sat., 08.00-13.00.
There are weekly markets in Quarteira on Wednesdays and Loulé on Saturdays. There are large monthly markets in some towns as follows:

Portimão	1st Monday
Alvor	2nd Tuesday
Odeaxere	4th Monday
Lagos	1st Saturday
Silves	3rd Monday
Almansil	1st & 4th Sunday
Albufeira	1st & 2rd Tuesday
Sagres	1st Friday

Medical Services:
There are medical centres in the larger resorts. For insurance purposes don't forget to obtain a receipt for any expenses. Some English-speaking doctors are:

Sagres (082) 789811/64173
Luz, Lagos, Alvor & Praia da Rocha (082) 798866/789811
Armacão de Pera (089) 588923
Albufeira 588923/586831/396157
Vilamoura and Quinta do Lago (089) 396157
Tavira (081) 971374

Post Offices:
Correios are identified by the letters CTT and there is one in most towns and even small villages. Opening hours are 09.00-12.00 and 14.00-18.00, Mon. to Fri. In Faro and Portimão the main post offices

are also open on Saturday morning. *Selos* or stamps can be bought at Tobacconists and some souvenir stands.

Shopping:
Opening hours are 09.00-13.00 and 15.00-19.00 Mon. to Fri. and 09.00-13.00 Sat.

Telephones:
Hotels make large surcharges so it is best to use call boxes which take 10, 20 and 50 *escudo* coins. An increasing number of call boxes accept phone cards which can be bought at post offices. To dial the UK: 00-44 + area code without the initial 0.

Toilets:
Very few public toilets exist except at railway stations and main bus stations. New museum buildings have them. Signs are often pictorial, but note the difference between *Senhores* (Men) and *Senoras* (Women). *Homens* is also used for Men.

Tourist Offices:
Most larger resorts have them and the opening hours are 09.30-12.30 and 14.00-17.30.

Transport:
Buses are quite cheap but not many services are of use to walkers. Between Lagos and Sagres buses can be used one way for three coastal walks. The following is a selection from the complete timetable.

Lagos	09.10	10.50	17.10	18.25*
Figueira	09.49	11.59	16.41	17.46*
Sagres	10.15	11.55	16.15	17.30*
	* Monday to Friday only			

Lagos and Salema is another useful service eg:

Lagos	09.00	Salema	16.48
Sr. de Luz	09.15	Budens	16.55
Burgau	09.22	B.S. Miguel	17.03

B.S. Miguel	09.35	Burgau	17.16
		Sr. de Luz	17.23
		Lagos	17.38

Trains are even cheaper than the buses but of limited use. There is a service between Lagos and Vila Real on the Spanish border, with stops at every station, making it a long journey. Some of the stations are a long way from the town they serve as at Albufeira. Those over 65 can buy concessionary tickets at 50% of the normal price, on production of their passport. Although travel by rail is slow, it is an interesting journey.

For those staying in Lagos the most useful train leaves at 09.35 reaching Mexilhoeira Grande at 09.46 (for Alvor estuary) and Portimão at 09.58 (for connection by bus to Monchique). This train does not arrive at Faro until 11.28. If you are near Faro a train leaves at 08.56 for Lagos, arriving 11.15. From Faro a train at 08.55 reaches Vila Real at 09.54 and one at 10.15 arrives 11.48.

Wildlife field trips
Full day field trips covering the nature reserves and other sites. Further information from John or Madge Measures, Quinta dos Almarjoes, Burgau, Algarve, Portugal. (0)82 69152.

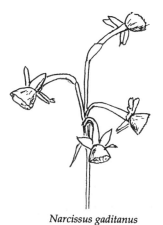

Narcissus gaditanus

CICERONE GUIDES
Cicerone publish a wide range of reliable guides to walking and climbing in Britain, and other general interest books.

LAKE DISTRICT - General Books
CONISTON COPPER A History
CHRONICLES OF MILNTHORPE
A DREAM OF EDEN
THE HIGH FELLS OF LAKELAND
LAKELAND - A taste to remember (Recipes)
LAKELAND VILLAGES
LAKELAND TOWNS
THE LOST RESORT? (Morecambe)
LOST LANCASHIRE (Furness area)
OUR CUMBRIA Stories of Cumbrian Men and Women
THE PRIORY OF CARTMEL
REFLECTIONS ON THE LAKES
AN ILLUSTRATED COMPANION INTO LAKELAND

LAKE DISTRICT - Guide Books
THE BORDERS OF LAKELAND
BIRDS OF MORECAMBE BAY
CASTLES IN CUMBRIA
CONISTON COPPER MINES Field Guide
THE CUMBRIA CYCLE WAY
THE EDEN WAY
IN SEARCH OF WESTMORLAND
SHORT WALKS IN LAKELND-1: SOUTH LAKELAND
SCRAMBLES IN THE LAKE DISTRICT
MORE SCRAMBLES IN THE LAKE DISTRICT
WALKING ROUND THE LAKES
WALKS IN SILVERDALE/ARNSIDE
WESTMORLAND HERITAGE WALK
WINTER CLIMBS IN THE LAKE DISTRICT

Northern England (outside the Lakes
BIRDWATCHING ON MERSEYSIDE
CANAL WALKS Vol 1 North
CANOEISTS GUIDE TO THE NORTH EAST
THE CLEVELAND WAY & MISSING LINK
THE DALES WAY
DOUGLAS VALLEY WAY
WALKING IN THE FOREST OF BOWLAND
HADRIANS WALL Vol 1 The Wall Walk
HERITAGE TRAILS IN NW ENGLAND
THE ISLE OF MAN COASTAL PATH
IVORY TOWERS & DRESSED STONES (Follies)
THE LANCASTER CANAL
LANCASTER CANAL WALKS
A WALKERS GUIDE TO THE LANCASTER CANAL
LAUGHS ALONG THE PENNINE WAY
A NORTHERN COAST-TO-COAST
NORTH YORK MOORS Walks
THE REIVERS WAY (Northumberland)
THE RIBBLE WAY
ROCK CLIMBS LANCASHIRE & NW
WALKING DOWN THE LUNE
WALKING IN THE SOUTH PENNINES
WALKING IN THE NORTH PENNINES
WALKING IN THE WOLDS
WALKS IN THE YORKSHIRE DALES (3 VOL)
WALKS IN LANCASHIRE WITCH COUNTRY
WALKS IN THE NORTH YORK MOORS
WALKS TO YORKSHIRE WATERFALLS (2 vol)
WATERFALL WALKS -TEESDALE & THE HIGH PENNINES
WALKS ON THE WEST PENNINE MOORS
WALKING NORTHERN RAILWAYS (2 vol)
THE YORKSHIRE DALES A walker's guide

Also a full range of EUROPEAN and OVERSEAS guidebooks - walking, long distance trails, scrambling, ice-climbing, rock climbing.

DERBYSHIRE & EAST MIDLANDS
KINDER LOG
HIGH PEAK WALKS
WHITE PEAK WAY
WHITE PEAK WALKS - 2 Vols
WEEKEND WALKS IN THE PEAK DISTRICT
THE VIKING WAY
THE DEVIL'S MILL / WHISTLING CLOUGH (Novels)

WALES & WEST MIDLANDS
ASCENT OF SNOWDON
WALKING IN CHESHIRE
CLWYD ROCK
HEREFORD & THE WYE VALLEY A Walker's Guide
HILLWALKING IN SNOWDONIA
HILL WALKING IN WALES (2 Vols)
THE MOUNTAINS OF ENGLAND & WALES Vol 1 WALES
WALKING OFFA'S DYKE PATH
THE RIDGES OF SNOWDONIA
ROCK CLIMBS IN WEST MIDLANDS
SARN HELEN Walking Roman Road
SCRAMBLES IN SNOWDONIA
SNOWDONIA WHITE WATER SEA & SURF
THE SHROPSHIRE HILLS A Walker's Guide
WALKING DOWN THE WYE
WELSH WINTER CLIMBS

SOUTH & SOUTH WEST ENGLAND
WALKING IN THE CHILTERNS
COTSWOLD WAY
COTSWOLD WALKS (3 VOLS)
WALKING ON DARTMOOR
WALKERS GUIDE TO DARTMOOR PUBS
EXMOOR & THE QUANTOCKS
THE KENNET & AVON WALK
LONDON THEME WALKS
AN OXBRIDGE WALK
A SOUTHERN COUNTIES BIKE GUIDE
THE SOUTHERN-COAST-TO-COAST
SOUTH DOWNS WAY & DOWNS LINK
SOUTH WEST WAY - 2 Vol
THE TWO MOORS WAY Dartmoor-Exmoor
WALKS IN KENT Bk 2
THE WEALDWAY & VANGUARD WAY

SCOTLAND
THE BORDER COUNTRY - WALKERS GUIDE
BORDER PUBS & INNS A Walker's Guide
CAIRNGORMS WINTER CLIMBS
WALKING THE GALLOWAY HILLS
THE ISLAND OF RHUM
THE SCOTTISH GLENS (Mountainbike Guide)
    Book 1:THE CAIRNGORM GLENS
    Book 2 THE ATHOLL GLENS
    Book 3 THE GLENS OF RANNOCH
SCOTTISH RAILWAY WALKS
SCRAMBLES IN LOCHABER
SCRAMBLES IN SKYE
SKI TOURING IN SCOTLAND
TORRIDON A Walker's Guide
WALKS from the WEST HIGHLAND RAILWAY
WINTER CLIMBS BEN NEVIS & GLENCOE

REGIONAL BOOKS UK & IRELAND
THE ALTERNATIVE PENNINE WAY
CANAL WALKS Vol.1: North
LIMESTONE - 100 BEST CLIMBS
THE PACKHORSE BRIDGES OF ENGLAND
THE RELATIVE HILLS OF BRITAIN
THE MOUNTAINS OF ENGLAND & WALES
    VOL 1 WALES, VOL 2 ENGLAND
THE MOUNTAINS OF IRELAND

Other guides are constantly being added to the Cicerone List.
Available from bookshops, outdoor equipment shops or direct (send s.a.e. for price list) from
CICERONE, 2 POLICE SQUARE, MILNTHORPE, CUMBRIA, LA7 7PY

CICERONE GUIDES

Cicerone publish a wide range of reliable guides to walking and climbing abroad

FRANCE, BELGIUM & LUXEMBOURG
CHAMONIX MONT BLANC - A Walking Guide
THE CORSICAN HIGH LEVEL ROUTE: GR20
FRENCH ROCK
THE PYRENEAN TRAIL: GR10
THE RLS (Stevenson) TRAIL
ROCK CLIMBS IN BELGIUM & LUXEMBOURG
ROCK CLIMBS IN THE VERDON
TOUR OF MONT BLANC
TOUR OF THE OISANS: GR54
TOUR OF THE QUEYRAS
WALKING THE FRENCH ALPS: GR5
WALKING THE FRENCH GORGES (Provence)
WALKS IN VOLCANO COUNTRY (Auvergne)
THE WAY OF ST JAMES: GR65

FRANCE / SPAIN
WALKS AND CLIMBS IN THE PYRENEES
ROCK CLIMBS IN THE PYRENEES

SPAIN
ANDALUSIAN ROCK CLIMBS
BIRDWATCHING IN MALLORCA
COSTA BLANCA CLIMBS
MOUNTAIN WALKS ON THE COSTA BLANCA
WALKING IN MALLORCA
WALKS & CLIMBS IN THE PICOS DE EUROPA
THE WAY OF ST JAMES: SPAIN

FRANCE / SWITZERLAND
CHAMONIX TO ZERMATT The Walker's Haute Route
THE JURA - Walking the High Route and Winter Ski
    Traverses

SWITZERLAND
THE ALPINE PASS ROUTE
THE BERNESE ALPS
CENTRAL SWITZERLAND
WALKS IN THE ENGADINE
WALKING IN TICINO
THE VALAIS - A Walking Guide

GERMANY / AUSTRIA / EASTERN EUROPE
HUT-TO-HUT IN THE STUBAI ALPS
THE HIGH TATRAS
THE KALKALPEN TRAVERSE
KING LUDWIG WAY
KLETTERSTEIG - Scrambles
MOUNTAIN WALKING IN AUSTRIA
WALKING IN THE BLACK FOREST
WALKING IN THE HARZ MOUNTAINS
WALKING IN THE SALZKAMMERGUT

ITALY & SLOVENIA
ALTA VIA - High Level Walks in the Dolomites
CLASSIC CLIMBS IN THE DOLOMITES
ITALIAN ROCK - Rock Climbs in Northern Italy
VIA FERRATA - Scrambles in the Dolomites
WALKING IN THE DOLOMITES
WALKS IN THE JULIAN ALPS

MEDITERRANEAN COUNTRIES
THE ATLAS MOUNTAINS
CRETE: Off the beaten track
THE MOUNTAINS OF GREECE
THE MOUNTAINS OF TURKEY
TREKS & CLIMBS IN WADI RUM, JORDAN
THE ALA DAG - Climbs & Treks (Turkey)

OTHER COUNTRIES
ADVENTURE TREKS - W. N. AMERICA
ANNAPURNA TREKKERS GUIDE
CLASSIC TRAMPS IN NEW ZEALAND
MOUNTAIN WALKING IN AFRICA 1: KENYA
ROCK CLIMBING IN HONG KONG
TREKKING IN THE CAUCAUSUS
TREKKING IN NEPAL
TREKKING - WESTERN NORTH AMERICA

GENERAL OUTDOOR BOOKS
THE ADVENTURE ALTERNATIVE
FIRST AID FOR HILLWALKERS
THE HILL WALKERS MANUAL
LIMESTONE -100 BEST CLIMBS IN BRITAIN
MOUNTAIN WEATHER
MOUNTAINEERING LITERATURE
MODERN ALPINE CLIMBING
MODERN SNOW & ICE TECHNIQUES
ROPE TECHNIQUES IN MOUNTAINEERING

CANOEING
CANOEIST'S GUIDE TO THE NORTH EAST
SNOWDONIA WILD WATER, SEA & SURF
WILDWATER CANOEING

CARTOON BOOKS
ON FOOT & FINGER
ON MORE FEET & FINGERS
LAUGHS ALONG THE PENNINE WAY
THE WALKERS

Also a full range of guidebooks
to walking, scrambling, ice-climbing,
rock climbing, and other adventurous
pursuits in Britain and abroad

Other guides are constantly being added to the Cicerone List.
Available from bookshops, outdoor equipment shops or direct (send for price list)
from CICERONE, 2 POLICE SQUARE, MILNTHORPE, CUMBRIA, LA7 7PY

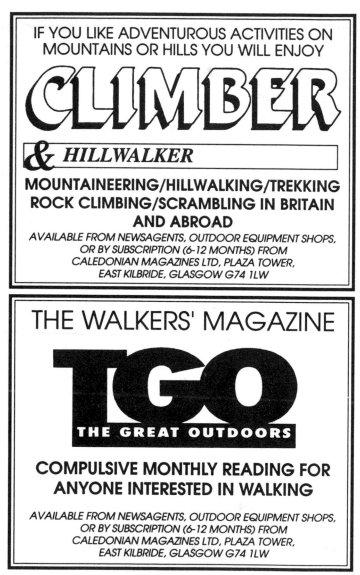